THE QUR'AN IN ISLAM

ITS IMPACT & INFLUENCE ON THE LIFE
OF MUSLIMS

By
`Allamah Sayyid M. H. Tabataba`i
Assadullah ad-Dhaakir Yate (Translator)

THE QUR'AN IN ISLAM

ITS IMPACT & INFLUENCE ON THE LIFE
OF MUSLIMS

By
`Allamah Sayyid M. H. Tabataba`i
Assadullah ad-Dhaakir Yate (Translator)

Zahra Publications

Publisher: Zahra Publications

ISBN-10 (Printed Version – Hardcover): 0-7103-0265-7

ISBN-13 (Printed Version – Hardcover): 978-0-7103-0265-6

ISBN-10 (Printed Version – Paperback): 0-7103-0266-5

ISBN-13 (Printed Version – Paperback): 978-0-7103-0266-3

ISBN (E-Book Version): 978-1-919826-86-8

http://www.zahrapublications.pub

First Print Edition Published in 1987

© Haeri Trust and Shaykh Fadhlalla Haeri

All rights reserved. Except for brief quotations in critical articles or reviews, no part of this Book may be reproduced in any manner without prior written permission from Zahra Publications.

Copying and redistribution of this Book is strictly prohibited.

Table of Contents

Book Description -- VI

Acknowledgements -------------------------------------- VII

Foreword -- VIII

Introduction --- XVI

Chapter 1

The Value of the Qur'an in the Eyes of the Muslims 1

Chapter 2

The Teachings of the Qur'an 11

Chapter 3

The Revelation of the Qur'an 61

Chapter 4

The Relationship of the Qur'an to the Sciences 89

Chapter 5

The Order of the Qur'an's Revelation and the Growth
of the Qur'anic Sciences.. 97

About

`Allamah Sayyid M. H. Tabataba`i 129

BOOK DESCRIPTION

From a general discussion of the Holy Qur'an's essential relevance to humanity, stressing God's guidance of all His creatures toward happiness and well-being, the author proceeds to show how the Qur'an contains the fundamental roots of Islam and the proof of prophethood as the Word of God. Copious quotations from the Qur'an are given to illustrate its teachings, its exoteric and esoteric dimensions and the meaning of exegesis. The eternal validity of Qur'anic revelation is examined in depth, together with the attitudes of both Muslim and non-Muslim writers to the questions of Revelation and Prophethood. The relationship of the Qur'an to the sciences shows to what extent it encourages us to study all manner of natural and physical sciences, as well as philosophy, literature and every available branch of knowledge. The book closes with a brief description of how the Qur'an has come down to us.

"THE QUR'AN IN ISLAM should be read now more than ever before because the current aberrations propagated in the name of Islam in general and Shi`ism in particular necessitate the uncompromising and clear statement of the traditional Islamic perspective as expounded by such masters as `Allamah Tabataba`i. Moreover, the present book marks an important addition to the literature in English on the central theophany of Islam, the Noble Qur'an."

– From the Foreword by Seyyed Hossein Nasr

ACKNOWLEDGEMENTS

We wish to express our thanks to all who contributed toward making this book possible: Assadullah ad-Dhaakir Yate, translation; David Elisha, editing; Seyyed Vali Reza Nasr, indexing; and Blue Cliff, cover design. Special gratitude is expressed to Seyyed Hossein Nasr for his contribution of the foreword to this book.

FOREWORD

Over a quarter of a century has passed since this book was written by `Allamah Tabataba`i in Persian – with the express purpose of being translated into English, as part of a trilogy whose aim was to make Shi`ism better known in the Western world[1]. Commissioned originally by Professor Kenneth Morgan of Colgate University in New York, who came to Iran with the aim of launching the project, this trilogy was written and assembled in a short period by `Allamah Tabataba`i in Persian and – in the case of the sayings of the Imams – Arabic. But it is only now, with the appearance of this translation, that the goal of the project is finally achieved, long after the author has left this abode of transience.

It was our task to collaborate with the `Allamah, to achieve the completion of the two works of this trilogy which he had set out to write himself, namely *Shi`ah dar Islam* and *Qur'an dar Islam*. Our role was to point out to this venerable master the questions which a Western audience needed to have treated and the types of discussion that such works needed to consider, while he himself set out to compose these books in his masterly and at the same time

---

1. The other two volumes in the trilogy, Shi`ite Islam, edited and translated by Seyyed Hossein Nasr, London, Allen & Unwin, and Albany, New York, SUNY Press, 1975; and A Shi`ite Anthology, selected and with a foreword by `Allamah Tabataba`i, translated with explanatory note by William Chittick and introduction by S. H. Nasr, London, Muhammadi Trust, and Albany, New York, SUNY Press, 1981, have already become well known as important sources in English for the study of Shi`ism.

unassuming style. Only after the composition of these works did he begin to select the sayings of the Imams which were to be collected and translated in the anthology.

The completion of *Shi`ah dar Islam* – after many journeys made by us between Tehran and Qum, where the `Allamah resided, as well as meetings in the cool mountain retreats surrounding Tehran – turned out to be a major event for the study of Shi`ism, not only in the West but also within Iran itself. Even before we completed the edition and translation of the work in English, the Persian edition with our humble introduction appeared in Iran, and soon became one of the most widely read works on Shi`ism. It seems that a work written with a Western audience in mind also bore a message of great significance for Shi`ites themselves.

While we were translating and editing *Shi`ite Islam*, `Allamah Tabataba`i terminated *Qur'an dar Islam*; on his advice, it was decided to have this also published in Persian as soon as possible. This work, likewise, became instantly popular and, like *Shi`ah dar Islam*, has gone into numerous editions besides being translated into other Islamic languages. Meanwhile, we began the translation of *Qur'an dar Islam* as soon as the publication of *Shi`ite Islam* in both its English and American editions was accomplished. Many sessions were spent with the `Allamah over various questions of translation, and the work progressed slowly because of both the `Allamah's busy program and our own crowded schedule. Over half of the work was translated when our library – and with it the manuscript of the translation – was lost during the events of 1979. It is, therefore, particularly gratifying finally to see the appearance of the translation of this work in English and the realization of the goal which was intended from the beginning.

The author of this book, `Allamah Sayyid Muhammad Husayn Tabataba`i – may God shower His blessings upon his soul – was one of the great masters of the traditional sciences in Iran during this century [20th century][2]. He was born in 1903 into a distinguished family of scholars in Tabriz, where he also carried out his earliest religious studies. Like many Shi`ite scholars, he pursued more advanced studies in Najaf and then returned to Tabriz. But in 1945, following the Soviet occupation of Azerbaijan, he came to Qum, where he settled until his death in 1982. From this centre of Shi`ite learning the light of his knowledge and presence began to disseminate, and continued to spread, among students not only of that city but also throughout Iran, and even beyond.

From the 1950s onward, his journeys to Tehran became a weekly or bi-weekly event, and he taught and conducted intellectual discussions with a small group of students, of which we had the honor of being one. This activity complemented his teaching activities in Qum. The circle in Tehran, which included not only such well-known Shi`ite scholars as Murtada Mutahhari, but also (during the fall season) Henry Corbin, and occasionally other Western scholars of Islam, helped to spread the influence of the `Allamah's teachings further, and soon he became recognized as one of the major intellectual figures of Shi`ism, at once master of the religious sciences (especially Qur'anic commentary), Islamic philosophy and gnosis (`irfan`).

Despite eye-problems which continued to hamper his activities to the very end, `Allamah Tabataba`i was an extremely prolific author. In addition to teaching throughout the week and training countless students, he wrote nearly

2. We have already dealt with his life in our preface to Shi`ite Islam, pp. 22-5.

every day, and important books and articles continued to flow from his pen. After writing such major philosophical works as *Usul-i Falsafay-i Ri'alism* in five volumes, he edited the *Asfar* of Sadr al-Din Shirazi with his own commentary, and a selection of commentaries on other masters prior to Shirazi, in seven volumes. Later, at our request, he composed two masterly summaries of Islamic philosophy: the *Badayi' al-Hikam* and the *Nahayat al-Hikam*.

Meanwhile, parallel with all this activity in the domain of traditional philosophy and gnosis (about which he wrote less in a direct manner but alluded to frequently in his philosophical works and certain shorter treatises), `Allamah Tabataba`i continued to work indefatigably on his Qur'anic commentary, *Tafsir al-Mizan*, which he finally completed in his mid-seventies. This monumental commentary, consisting of some twenty-seven volumes (written in Arabic, but also translated into Persian), is one of the most important Qur'anic commentaries of this century and is a blinding witness to the remarkable mastery of its author in the domain of Qur'anic sciences. This commentary, based on the principle of having one part of the Qur'an interpret other parts (*al-Qur'an yufassiru ba`dahu ba`dan*), is a *summa* of Islamic religious thought, in which the sciences of the Qur'an, theology, philosophy, gnosis, sacred history and the social teachings of Islam are all brought together.

The present volume is in a sense the synthesis of the venerable master's life-long study of the Noble Qur'an, Although the book is written in a simple language and may appear to be introductory, it is a work of great depth and synthetic quality. It treats many questions concerning the sacred text which have rarely been discussed together in a single work. The book, although short, distils many volumes into its pages and is like the synopsis of a major commentary. It brings out the significances of the Qur'an for the life of Muslims, the features of the sacred text which seem enigmatic, the inner and outer levels of meaning of the Text and the sciences of Qur'anic exegesis. It also treats in a clear and direct manner the Shi`ite understanding of the Qur'an and the role of the Imams in its interpretation. It is a veritable prolegomenon to the study of the Sacred Book, and is perhaps the most accessible introduction available in English to the study of the Qur'an as traditionally understood by the mainstream of Shi`ite thought, in fact Islamic exegetical thought in general.

This book reflects, moreover, not only the learning of the author but also his spiritual qualities. `Allamah Tabataba`i was not only an outstanding scholar but also a person of great spiritual realization who lived constantly in the remembrance of God. During the twenty years during which we had the honor of being his student, and observing him in all kinds of circumstances – from being alone with him in a room, to sitting at his feet in a mosque filled with hundreds of students – never did he cease to remember God and invoke Him. His countenance always reflected a light which seemed to shine from the world beyond, while his gentle voice seemed to issue from the other shore of existence. In his presence, one could not but think of God and the world of the Spirit. The reality of the Qur'an, which he had studied and written about for so many years, seemed to have penetrated into his very being, enabling him to speak of a knowledge that was always wed to spirituality and rooted in the sacred.

`Allamah Tabataba`i was at once one of the greatest of Qur'anic commentators, a leading contemporary Islamic philosopher in the tradition of Ibn Sina, Suhrawardi and Mulla Sadra, and a gnostic who was at home in both the metaphysical works of Ibn `Arabi and the inebriating poetry of Rumi and Hafiz. In him, intelligence, scholarship, piety and the love of God met in a union which is encountered rarely in any age, and especially this period of the eclipse of the Spirit. His soul was embellished with the virtues extolled by the Qur'an and the prophetic *Sunnah*, while his mind explored like a soaring eagle the vast expanses of Islamic thought. To have met him was to have met the veritable Islamic scholar (or `*alim*), and to gain a taste of what traditional Islamic learning must have been when the whole of the Islamic intellectual tradition was fully alive.

The *Qur'an in Islam*, as well as the other works by the `Allamah, should be read now more than ever before, because the current aberrations propagated in the name of Islam in general, and Shi`ism in particular, necessitate an uncompromising and clear statement of the traditional Islamic perspective, as expounded by such masters as `Allamah Tabataba`i. Moreover, the present book marks an important addition to literature in English on the central theophany of Islam, the Noble Qur'an. May all those interested in the understanding of Islam be able to benefit from this book, and also come to gain some insight into the mind and soul of a great contemporary Muslim scholar who lived and died in constant awareness of God, and who saw in His Word as contained in the Noble Book at once a guide for life, the basic source of all knowledge, the sword of discernment between truth and falsehood and a "presence" whose experience makes possible here a taste of the realities of paradise.

Seyyed Hossein Nasr
Bethesda, Maryland
December, 1986

INTRODUCTION

We are placing before the reader a book which discusses the profoundest document of the sacred religion of Islam. Among the themes of this book are the following:

- The position of the Glorious Qur'an in the Islamic world
- What do we mean when we speak of "the Qur'an?"
- What value does the Qur'an hold for Muslims?
- The Qur'an as a book whose importance is global and eternal
- The Qur'an as a revelation from a divine, not a human, source
- The relationship between the Qur'an and the sciences
- The characteristics and features of the Qur'an

We are investigating the importance of a book which Muslims have never ceased to respect and venerate and whose validity they have never rejected. They are able to use it to support any claim made in the name of Islam, despite being troubled by inner conflicts and sectarian splintering, as are the other major world religions.

The purpose of this work is to define the position of the Qur'an in such a way that the Holy Book explains itself, rather than merely giving our own opinions concerning it.

There is clearly a great difference between these two ways of approaching the matter.

In other words, the position we attribute to the Holy Qur'an, through reason or lack of it, if found to be contrary to the Qur'anic views, will not be valid. If it is something about which the Qur'an is silent, in view of the existing differences of opinion among the Muslims, a unanimous acceptance of such a view would not be possible. The only position which may be acceptable is what is denoted by the Holy Qur'an itself.

Therefore, in this inquiry and discussion, we must answer the question as to what the Holy Qur'an says in this connection, and not what we, who follow a certain school of Islamic law, say about the Holy Qur'an.

Chapter 1

THE VALUE OF THE QUR'AN IN THE EYES OF THE MUSLIMS

The Qur'an Contains a Pattern of a Complete Way of Life for Man

The religion of Islam is superior to any other in that it guarantees happiness in man's life. For Muslims, Islam is a belief system with moral and practical laws that have their source in the Qur'an.

God, may He be exalted, says, *"Indeed this Qur'an guides to the path which is clearer and straighter than any other"* [17:9]. He also says, *"We have revealed to you the book which clarifies every matter"* [16:89].

These references exemplify the numerous Qur'anic verses (*ayaat*) which mention the principles of religious belief, moral virtues and a general legal system governing all aspects of human behavior.

A consideration of the following topics will enable one to understand that the Qur'an provides a comprehensive program of activity for man's life.

Man has no other aim in life but the pursuit of happiness and pleasure, which manifests itself in much the same way as love of ease or wealth. Although some individuals seem to reject this happiness, for example, by ending their lives in suicide, or by turning away from a life of leisure, they too, in their own way, confirm this principle of happiness; for, in seeking an end to their life or of material pleasure, they are still asserting their own personal choice of what happiness means to them. Human actions, therefore, are directed largely by the prospects of happiness and prosperity offered by a certain idea, whether that idea be true or false.

Man's activity in life is guided by a specific plan or program. This fact is self-evident, even though it is sometimes concealed by its very apparentness. Man acts according to his will and desires; he also weighs the necessity of a task before undertaking it.

In this he is promoted by an inherent scientific law, which is to say that he performs a task for "himself" in fulfilling needs which he perceives are necessary. There is, therefore, a direct link between the objective of a task and its execution.

Any action undertaken by man, whether it be eating, sleeping or walking, occupies its own specific place and demands its own particular efforts. Yet an action is implemented according to an inherent law, the general concept of which is stored in man's perception and is recalled by motions associated with that action. This notion holds true whether or not one is obliged to undertake the action or whether or not the circumstances are favorable.

Every man, in respect of his own actions, is as the state in relation to its individual citizens, whose activity is controlled by specific laws, customs and behavior. Just as the active forces in a state are obliged to adapt their actions according to certain laws, so is the social activity of a community composed of the actions of each individual. If this were not the case, the different components of society would fall apart and be destroyed in anarchy in the shortest time imaginable.

If a society is religious, its government will reflect that religion; if it is secular, it will be regulated by a corresponding code of law. If a society is uncivilized and barbaric, a code of behavior imposed by a tyrant will appear; otherwise, the conflict of various belief-systems within such a society will produce lawlessness.

Thus man, as an individual element of society, has no option but to possess and pursue a goal. He is guided in the pursuit of his goal by the path which corresponds to it and by the rules which must necessarily accompany his program of activity. The Qur'an affirms this idea when it says that *"every man has a goal to which he is turning, so compete with each other in good action"* [2:148]. In the usage of the Qur'an, the word *deen*[3] is basically applied to a way, a pattern of living, and neither the believer nor the non-believer is without a path, be it prophetic or man-made.

God, may He be exalted, describes the enemies of the divine *deen* (religion) as those *"who prevent others from the path of God and would have it crooked"* [7:45]

This verse shows that the term *Sabil Allah* – the path of God – used in the verse refers to the *deen of fitrah* – the inherent pattern of life intended by God for man. It also indicates that even those who do not believe in God implement His *deen*, albeit in a deviated form; this deviation, which becomes their *deen*, is also encompassed in God's program.

---

3. Usually translated to mean religion, the word strongly implies transaction between the Debtor (God) and the indebted (man). Hence, living the *deen* means repaying one's debt to the Creator.

The best and firmest path in life for man is the one which is dictated by his innate being and not by the sentiments of any individual or society. A close examination of any part of creation reveals that, from its very inception, it is guided by an innate purpose towards fulfilling its nature along the most appropriate and shortest path; every aspect of each part of creation is equipped to do so, acting as a blueprint for defining the nature of its existence. Indeed all of creation, be it animate or inanimate, is made up in this manner.

As an example, we may say that a green-tipped shoot, emerging from a single grain in the earth, is "aware" of its future existence as a plant which will yield an ear of wheat. By means of its inherent characteristics, the shoot acquires various mineral elements for its growth from the soil and changes, day by day, in form and strength until it becomes a fully-matured grain-bearing plant – and so comes to the end of its natural cycle.

Similarly, if we investigate the life-cycle of the walnut tree, we observe that it too is "aware", from the very beginning, of its own specific purpose in life, namely, to grow into a big walnut tree. It reaches this goal by developing according to its own distinct inherent characteristics; it does not, for example, follow the path of the wheat-plant in fulfilling its goal just as the wheat-plant does not follow the life pattern of the walnut tree.

Since every created object which makes up the visible world is subject to this same general law, there is no reason to doubt that man, as a species of creation, is not. Indeed his physical capabilities are the best proof of this rule; like the rest of creation, they allow him to realize his purpose, and ultimate happiness, in life.

Thus, we observe that man, in fact, guides himself to happiness and well-being merely by applying the fundamental laws inherent in his own nature.

This law is confirmed by God in the Qur'an, through His Prophet Moses, when he says, *"Our Lord is He who gave everything its nature, then guided it"* [20:50]. It is further explained in 87:2-3 as *"He who created and fashioned in balanced proportion and He who measures and guides"*.

As to the creation and the nature of man, the Qur'an says,

By the soul and Him who fashioned it and then inspired it [to know] its wrong action and fear of God and fear of God; he is truly successful who causes it to grow and purifies it and he is a failure who corrupts and destroys it [91:7-10].

God enjoins upon man the duty to *"strive towards a sincere application of the deen,"* (that is, the *fitrah* of God, or the natural code of behavior upon which He has created mankind), since *"there is no changing (the laws of) the creation of God"* [30:30].

He also says that *"In truth, the only* deen *recognized by God is Islam"* [3:19]. Here, Islam means submission, the method of submission to these very laws. The Qur'an further warns that *"the actions of the man who chooses a* deen *other than Islam will not be accepted"* [3:85].

The gist of the above verses, and other references on the same subject, is that God has guided every creature – be it man, beast or vegetable – to a state of well-being and self-fulfillment appropriate to its individual make-up.

Thus the appropriate path for man lies in the adoption of personal and social laws particular to his own *fitrah* (or innate nature), and in avoiding people who have become "denaturalized" by following their own notions or passions. It is clearly underlined that *fitrah*, far from denying man's feelings and passions, accords each its proper due and allows man's conflicting spiritual and material needs to be fulfilled in a harmonious fashion.

Thus, we may conclude that the intellect, `aql, should rule man in matters pertaining to individual or personal decisions, rather than his feelings. Similarly, truth and justice should govern society and not the whim of a tyrant or even the will of a majority, if that be contrary to a society's true benefit.

From this we may conclude that only God is empowered to make laws, since the only laws useful to man are those which are made according to his inherent nature.

It also follows that man's needs, arising from his outward circumstance and his inner reality, are fulfilled only by obeying God's instructions (or laws). These needs may arise through events beyond man's control or as a result of the natural demands of his body.

Both are encompassed in the plan of life that God has designated for man. For, as the Qur'an says, the *"decision rests with God only,"* [12:40 and 67] which is to say that there is no governance (of man or society, of the inner or the outer) except that of God.

Without a specific creational plan, based on the innate disposition of man, life would be fruitless and without meaning. We may understand this only through belief in God and knowledge of his Unity, as explained in the Qur'an.

From here we may proceed to an understanding of the Day of Judgment, when man is rewarded or punished according to his deeds. Thereafter, we may arrive at knowledge of the prophets and of prophetic teachings, since man cannot be judged without being first instructed in the matter of obedience and disobedience. These three fundamental teachings are considered to be the roots of the Islamic way of life.

To these we may add the fundamentals of good character and morals which a true believer must possess, and which are a necessary extension of the three basic beliefs mentioned above. The laws governing daily activity not only guarantee man's happiness and moral character but, more importantly, increase his understanding of these beliefs and of the fundamentals of Islam.

It is clear that a thief, a traitor, a squanderer or a libertine do not possess the quality of innocence; nor can a miser, who hoards money, be called a generous person. Similarly, someone who never prays or remembers God cannot be called a believer in God and the Last Day, nor be described as His servant.

From this we may conclude that good character flourishes when joined to a pattern of correct actions; morals are to be found in the man whose beliefs are in harmony with these fundamentals. A proud man cannot be expected to believe in God nor be humble in respect to the Divine; nor can the man, who has never understood the meaning of humanity, justice, mercy or compassion, believe in the Day of Rising and the Judgment.

Chapter 35:10 speaks of the relationship between a sincere system of belief and a fitting character:

Pure speech rises up to Him and He raises up good deeds still further.

In chapter 30:10 we learn again of this relationship between belief and action:

> *Then evil was the consequence of those who do wrong action because they denied the signs of Allah and they made a mock of them.*

To summarize, the Qur'an is composed of the following Islamic fundamentals which together form an interlocking whole: a primary system of belief in the Unity of God, Prophethood and the Day of Reckoning, accompanied by a second group of beliefs, namely, belief in the Tablet, the Pen (which delineates the sequence of cosmic events), the rule of destiny and the decree (without implying pre-determination)[4], the angels, the throne of the Creator, and, finally, in the creation of the sky, the earth and everything between them.

Thereafter, we observe that man's well-being lies in his character being in harmony with these principles.

The *shari`ah*, namely the laws and code of behavior explained in the Qur'an and commented upon in every detail by the model of the Prophet's life, is the means whereby a man may practice these principles. At this point we should add that the Prophet's family are his chosen heirs and are entrusted with the task of exemplifying and explaining further the prophetic message and the *shari`ah* after the Prophet's death. The Prophet himself has shown that the tradition, *hadith*[5], known as the *hadith al-thaqalayn* which all sects of Islam accept, refers specifically to this matter of succession.

---

4. Please see our publication: *Decree & Destiny*.

5. A report of the words or deeds of the Prophet which has been transmitted to us intact by a chain, or numerous chains, of trustworthy narrators. The tradition in question here possesses an unbroken chain of transmission back to the Prophet himself; these verses confirm the miraculous quality of the book and state that it is beyond the power of man to produce such a work.

The Qur'an as a Document of Prophethood

The Qur'an refers on several occasions to the fact that it is the word of God, that it issues from a divine source in the very words in which the Prophet received them and which he later transmitted. The divine nature of the Qur'an is affirmed in several verses.

In 52:33-34 we read, *"or they say that (the Prophet) is inventing it. Indeed they do not believe. If they are truthful then let them produce words like it"*. Likewise in 17:88 *"Say (O Muhammad), if all the jinn and mankind were to join forces to produce something like this Qur'an they could not produce it even if they were to help one another."* Again, in 11:13 *"or they say he has invented it! Say: then produce ten verses like it which you have invented,"* and again in 10:38, *"or they say he has invented it. Say; produce a single chapter like it,"* we find further proof.

The following challenge is made in Chapter 2:23 *"and if you are in doubt concerning that which We have revealed to Our slave then produce a chapter like it."*

Here it should be noted that the Qur'an is addressing those who grew up with Muhammad, the man they knew to be unlettered and untutored in the matters spoken about in the Qur'an. Despite this knowledge, they still doubt.

Another challenge is issued, (to those who would find contradictions in the Qur'an, but obviously cannot):

> *Will they not reflect upon the Qur'an? If it had been from other than God, they would have found in it much incongruity [4:82].*

Since everything in the world is in a state of growth and self-perfection, then the Qur'an would of necessity lack harmony since it was revealed over a period of twenty-three years - it would lack harmony; that is, if we were to suppose that it was the work of a man rather than of God. The Qur'an, whose messages announce and confirm that it is the work of God, also teaches us that Muhammad is a messenger, sent by God, thus confirming the authenticity of the Prophet. In chapter 13:43 God speaks Himself, as on many occasions, confirming that He is witness and testimony to the prophecy of Muhammad: *"Say: God is sufficient witness between you and me."* The verse refers to disbelievers and defies their disbelief.

In another verse, the testimony of angels is added to that of God's:

> *"But God testifies concerning that which He has revealed to you; He has revealed it in His knowledge; and the Angels also testify. And God is sufficient witness [4:166].*

Chapter 2

THE TEACHINGS OF THE QUR'AN

The Universal Import of the Qur'an

The Qur'an is not directed towards any one particular nation, such as the Arabs, or to a particular sect of Muslims, but to non-Islamic societies as well as the Muslim nation as a whole. There are numerous references to non-believers and idol-worshippers, to the People of the Book (namely, the Jews, or the Tribe of Israel, and the Christians), exhorting each one to strive towards a true understanding of the Qur'an and of Islam.

The Qur'an calls each group to Islam by providing proofs and never stipulates that they be of Arab stock. Referring to idol-worshippers, God says, *"if they repent and establish worship and pay the poor-due, then they are your brothers in religion"* [9:11].

Likewise, God talks about the People of the Book, (Jews, Christians and we include here the Zoroastrians), without referring to them as Arabs:

> *Say, O People of the Book come to an agreement between us and you: that we shall worship none but God and*

> *that we shall ascribe no partners to Him and that none of us shall take others for lords beside God [3:64].*

It is true that before Islam spread beyond the Arabian Peninsula, Qur'anic injunctions were obviously directed towards the Arab nation. From the sixth year after the *hijrah* (the migration of the Prophet from Mecca to Medina), when the *deen* of Islam was being propagated beyond the peninsula, there are references which demonstrate that the Qur'an is addressing itself to mankind in general; for example, in 6:19, *"this Qur'an has been revealed to me that I may warn you and whomever it may reach,"* and in 68:52 God says, *"it is nothing else but a reminder to the worlds."*

We read too in 74:35-36, *"In truth this is one of the greatest signs, being a warning unto men."*

History has amply demonstrated that Islam has been embraced by a number of leading members of other religions, including the idol-worshippers of Mecca, Jews, Christians and by people from diverse communities, such as Salman of Persia, Suhayb from the Roman people, and Bilal of Ethiopia.

The Perfection of the Qur'an

The Qur'an shows man the way to a realization of his goal on earth; it describes this path in the most complete terms. It is a way of correctly viewing the reality of things; a vision – personal, social and cosmic – based on a correct manner of behavior and a precise method of interaction between men.

In 46:30 we read that the Qur'an *"guides to the truth and a right road,"* meaning the road of right belief and correct action. On another occasion, mentioning the Torah and the New Testament, God says, *"We have revealed this Book to you with the Truth, confirming whatever Book was before it, and We keep watch over it"* [5:48].

The Qur'an thus affirms the truth of the ways of guidance taught by the earlier prophets. In chapter 42:13, *"He has ordained for you that religion which He commended to Noah and that which We reveal to you (Muhammad) and that We commended to Abraham, Moses and Jesus,"* and in chapter 16:89, *"And We revealed the book to you as an exposition of all things."*

Thus we understand from these verses that the Qur'an not only encompasses the meanings and teachings of all divine books revealed before it, but also adds to and completes them. Every thing which a man needs, both in terms of his spiritual and his social life, is contained and explained in the Qur'an.

The Eternal Quality of the Qur'an

The perfection and completeness of the Qur'an prove that its validity is not restricted to a particular time or place, since anything perfect is in need of nothing to complete it.

In chapter 86:13-14 God confirms that the Qur'an is *"a conclusive word"* and not a mere *"pleasantry."* It contains the purest of teachings concerning belief in life-after-death, together with an exposition of the realities of existence, while, at the same time, encompassing the fundamentals of correct human behavior.

Since laws governing transactions between men are directly linked to their beliefs, such a book can obviously not be annulled or changed with the passage of time. As He says in 17:105, *"We have revealed the Qur'an with Truth and it has descended with the Truth,"* meaning that the revelations and their ongoing validity are inseparable from the Truth.

Thus in 10:32, *"After the Truth what is there except error,"* and in 41:41-42, *"In truth it is an unpenetrable book, error may not enter in it from before it or behind it."*

In other words the Qur'an repulses, by its own perfection and completeness, any attempt to alter it; and neither now nor later can it be annulled or superseded. Many studies have been made of the permanence of the validity of the laws given in the Qur'an.

The reader is advised to consult them if he requires additional knowledge of the subject; to pursue the matter here, (namely, the position of the Qur'an in the lives of Muslims and the manner in which it demonstrates this), would be outside the scope of this book.

The Qur'an as a Self-Contained Proof

The Qur'an, being composed of words and meanings like any other book, explains itself. It does not remain silent when the situation of the text demands proof. Moreover, there is no reason to believe that Qur'anic terms mean anything other than the actual words being used. This means that every man, possessing a certain knowledge of the Arabic language, may clearly understand the meaning of the Qur'an just as he understands any other words written in Arabic.

There are many verses which are directed towards a specific group, such as the Tribe of Israel, or the Believers, or the non-believers and, sometimes, man in general; (they are addressed in phrases such as *"O you who disbelieve"* or *"O people of the Book"* or *"O tribe of Israel"* or *"O Mankind"*). The Qur'an discourses with them, offering them proof of its validity or challenging them to produce a book similar to it if they doubt it to be the Word of God.

Obviously it makes no sense to address people in terms which they do not understand or to demand that they produce something similar to that which has no meaning for them. In chapter 47:24 we read, *"Why do they not reflect upon the Qur'an,"* implying that if it was from other than God, people would have found in it many inconsistencies.

It is clearly indicated in the Qur'an that verses which have a subtlety or particularity of meaning demand that the reader reflect upon them to remove any seeming differences of interpretation or incongruities that may appear at first inspection.

It also follows that if the verses themselves contained no apparent meaning, there would be no point in reflecting upon them in order to clarify the apparent problem of their interpretation. There are no indications from other sources, (such as the traditions of the Prophet), that demand a rejection of the outwardly manifest meaning of the Qur'an.

Some have argued that one should only refer to the commentaries of the Prophet in elucidating the meanings of the Qur'an. This argument is unacceptable, however, since the basis of the Prophet's commentary and of the Imams of his family must be sought for in the Qur'an.

It is difficult to imagine that the validity of the Qur'an is dependent on the commentaries of the Prophet or the Imams of his family. Rather, affirmation of prophecy and imamate must be contained in the Qur'an, which itself is the authentic proof and document of prophecy. This does not, however, contradict the fact that the Prophet and the Imams of his family were responsible for clarifying those details of the *shari`ah* law (Divinely revealed law) which were not apparent from the actual text of the Qur'an.

They were, likewise, entrusted with teaching the knowledge contained in the Book, as seen in the following verse:

And We have revealed to you the Remembrance so that you may explain to mankind that which has been revealed for them [16:44].

A similar reflection occurs in chapter 59:7 where, in reference to the code of practice and law brought by the Prophet to mankind, it states, *"And take whatever the messenger gives you. And abstain from whatever he forbids."*

In chapter 4:64 it says, *"We sent no messenger save that he should be obeyed by God's leave"* and, again, in chapter 62:2, *"He it is who has sent among the unlettered ones a messenger of their own, to recite to them His revelations and to make them grow and to teach them the Book and Wisdom."* According to these verses, the Prophet is the appointed explainer of the details of the *shari`ah* law as well as the teacher of the Qur'an.

Moreover, according to the tradition known as *thaqalayn*, which was authenticated by an uninterrupted chain of narrators, the Prophet has appointed the Imams of his own family as his successors. This is not to deny that others also, by correctly applying the learnings of sincere teachers, may understand the meaning of the Qur'an.

The Inner and Outer Dimensions of the Qur'an

In chapter 4:36 God says, *"And serve God and ascribe nothing as a partner to Him."* The verse prohibits pre-Islamic Arabs from their worship of idols, just as chapter 22:30 urges them to *"shun the filth of idols, and shun lying speech."* On reflection it becomes clear that an idol may exist in any form; therefore, idol-worship is forbidden because it involves submission to an entity other than God.

In chapter 36:60 God treats the devil as an idol when He says, *"Did I not charge you, O you sons of Adam, that you do not worship the devil."* It also becomes clear that another form of idol-worship is submission to one's desires or to the will of others, over and above the will of God; this is indicated in 45:23 which refers to *"him who makes his desire his God."*

Thus it becomes apparent that one should turn to none other for help than God Himself and not forget Him in any circumstances, since to do otherwise would be to direct one's attention away from God. To submit to others is to belittle Him and this is the very essence of idol-worship. Thus, in chapter 7:179 God says of those who refused to worship Him, *"Already We have urged into hell many of the jinn and humankind, . . . These are the neglectful."* The verse, *"ascribe nothing to Him,"* clearly forbids worships of idols; that is to say, man may not, without God's permission, submit himself to others including his own desires, since any such submission would render him neglectful of God.

In this way, the simple, apparent text of the verse unfolds multiple meanings and exemplifies a feature to be found throughout the Qur'an. Thus the saying of the Prophet, (related in the books of hadith and commentary), become clear:

> *In truth the Qur'an possesses an inner and outer, and the inner contains seven dimensions*[6].

---

6. See al-Fayd al-Kashani, *al-Safi fi tafsir al-Qur'an*, pp. 38-41; `Abbas al-Qummi, *Safinat al-bihar*, s.v. "Batn".

The Wisdom Contained in the Two Facets of the Qur'an: The Inner and the Outer

Man's primary life, namely, the temporal life of this world, is as a bubble on the immense sea of the material; and since all his transactions concern the material, he is throughout his life, at the mercy of the moving waves. All his senses are occupied with the material and his thoughts influenced by sensory information. Eating, drinking, standing, speaking, listening, like all other human actions, take place in the sphere of the material and not in the sphere of thought.

Moreover, in reflecting upon such concepts as love, enmity, ambition and nobility, one comes to better understand them by translating them into language derived from the senses or from actual material objects; for example, the magnetic attraction of lovers, a burning ambition, or a man's being a mine of wisdom.

Capacity to comprehend the world of meaning, which is vaster than that of the material, varies from man to man. For one person it may be almost impossible to imagine the world of meanings; another may perceive it only in the most superficial terms and, yet another, may comprehend with ease the most profound of spiritual concepts.

One may say that the greater a man's capacity to understand meanings, the lesser he is attached to the world of the material and its alluring, deceiving appearance. By his very nature, each person possesses a potential for understanding meanings and, provided that he does not deny this capacity, it may be cultivated and increased further.

It is not a simple matter to reduce meaning from one level of understanding to another without losing its sense. This is particularly true for meanings possessing great subtlety which cannot be transmitted, especially to ordinary people, without adequate explanation. As one example, we may mention the Hindu religion: anyone reflecting deeply upon the Vedic scriptures of India and studying the different aspects of its message will ultimately see that its basic aim is the worship of one God.

Unfortunately this aim is explained in such a complicated manner that the concept of oneness reaches the minds of ordinary people in the form of idol-worship and the recognition of many gods. To avoid such problems, it becomes necessary to communicate meanings hidden beyond the material world in a language which is rooted in the material and readily comprehensible world.

Indeed some religions deprive their adherents of rights accorded to them by the religion itself; women, for example, in Hinduism; Jews and Christians who, in general, are denied access to knowledge of their holy books. Islam does not deprive anyone of their rights in the *deen*, and both man and woman, scholar and layman, black and white are equal in being accorded access to their religion.

God affirms this in chapter 3:195, *"Indeed I do not allow the work of any worker, male or female, to be lost,"* and, again, in chapter 49:13, *"O mankind! Truly we have created you male and female and have made you nations and tribes that you may know one another. Indeed the noblest of you in the sight of God is the best in conduct."*

In this manner the Qur'an addresses its teachings to mankind at large and affirms that every man may increase himself in knowledge and, thereby, perfect his own behavior. In fact, the Qur'an addresses its teachings specifically to the world of man. Since, as mentioned earlier, each man has a different capacity of understanding and since the expounding of subtle knowledge is not without danger of misinterpretation, the Qur'an directs its teachings primarily at the level of the common man.

In this manner, the subtlest of meanings can be explained and multiple meanings and ideas expressed, to the ordinary person, by co-relating them to concrete sensory meanings; meaning, therefore, is always inherent in the letter of the words.

The Qur'an reveals itself in a way suitable for different levels of comprehension so that each benefits according to his own capacity. In chapter 43:3-4 God emphasizes this idea:

Truly we have appointed it a lecture in Arabic so that you may perhaps understand and indeed in the source of the Book, which we possess, it is sublime, decisive.

God describes the different capacities of man's comprehension in the following metaphor in chapter 13:17:

He sends down water from the sky, so that valleys flow according to their measure;

"and the Prophet, in a famous tradition[7] says; "We prophets talk to the people according to the capacity of their intellects."

Another result of the multiple meanings within the Qur'an is that the verses take on a significance beyond their immediate text. Certain verses contain metaphors which indicate divine gnosis far beyond the common man's understanding but which, nevertheless, become comprehensible through their metaphorical form.

---

7. Muhammad Baqir al-Majlisi, *Bihar al-anwar*, vol. 1, p. 37.

God says in chapter 17:89, *"And indeed We have displayed for mankind in this Qur'an all kinds of similitudes, but most of mankind refuse everything except disbelief."* And again in chapter 29:43 God talks of metaphors as a means of expression, *"As for these similitudes, We coin them for mankind, but none will grasp their meanings except those of knowledge."*

Consequently, we must conclude that all Qur'anic teachings which deal with subtle profound knowledge, are in the form of similitudes.

The Two Kinds of Qur'anic Verses: The Explicit and the Implicit

In chapter 11:1 God says of the Qur'an, *"This is a book whose meanings are secure."* From this we may draw the meaning to read *"whose meanings are perfected, expanded, firm and strong."* In chapter 39:23, it reads,

> *God has revealed the fairest of statements (consistent with and in relation to each other) and arranged in pairs (according to meaning) which cause the flesh of those who fear their Lord to creep.*

In chapter 3:7 He says, *"He it is who has revealed to you the Book in which are clear revelations,* (that is, verses whose meaning is immediately clear and which Muslims use for guidance).

> *They are the substance of the Book and others which are allegorical. But those in whose heart is doubt indeed follow the allegorical seeking dissension by seeking to explain it. None knowest its explanation except God and those who are of sound instruction say: We believe in it, it is all from our Lord.*

The first of the verses describes those sections of the Qur'an whose meaning is explicit, clear and unambiguous, and safe from misinterpretation. The second verse refers to all those verses whose meanings are implicit, and which are considered allegorical. It then proceeds to indicate that both types of verses, (the explicit, or clear and the implicit, or allegorical), share certain common qualities: beauty and sweetness of language, and a miraculous power of expression which are present in the entire Qur'an.

The third verse under consideration divides the Qur'an into two parts: the explicit and the implicit, the clear and the allegorical, or, in Qur'anic terms, the *muhkam* and the *mutashabih*.

The *muhkam* and those verses which are explicit, clear and immediate in their message and, therefore, incapable of being misinterpreted; the *mutashabih* verses are not of this nature. It is the duty of every firm believer to believe in and act according to the verses which are *muhkam*.

It is also his duty to believe in the verses which are *mutashabih*, but he must abstain from acting upon them; this injunction is based on the premise that only those whose heart is corrupt and whose belief is false follow the implicit, *mutashabih*, verses, fabricating interpretations and, thereby, deceiving common people.

The Meanings of the Explicit and the Implicit Verses, According to the Commentators and Scholars

There is much difference of opinion amongst the Islamic scholars concerning the meaning of explicit and implicit verses, with almost twenty different views on the matter. We can, however, conclude from the views of commentators, ranging from the time of the Prophet to the present day, that the explicit verses are clear and unambiguous, and that one is obliged to believe in and act according to them.

The implicit verses, on the other hand, are those which outwardly seem to express a meaning, but which contain a further truer meaning whose interpretation is known only to God; man has no access to it. However, he is enjoined to believe in them but to avoid acting upon them.

This view is held amongst the Sunni scholars. It is also maintained by the Shi`ite scholars except they believe that the Prophet and the Imams of his family also understood the hidden meanings. They also maintain that the ordinary man must seek knowledge of the implicit verses from God, the Prophet and the Imams.

This view, although held by most commentators, is in several aspects not in accord with the text of the verse beginning,

> *He it is who has revealed to you the Book in which are explicit verses (whose meanings are immediately clear) . . .*

The Method of Guidance and Explanation Used in the Rest of the Qur'an

This we may attribute, firstly, to the fact that there is no verse whose meaning is totally obscure since the Qur'an describes itself as a light, as a guidance and as an explanation. Thus it is not befitting that there be verses which fail to reveal their meaning, or to illuminate the Qur'an as a whole.

We should examine again the verse,

Will they not ponder on the Qur'an? If it had been from other than God they would have found much inconsistency in it [4:82].

Thus reflection on the Qur'an would remove all kinds of seeming inconsistencies making it unacceptable to say, as do most of the scholars, that the implicit verses cannot be totally understood and that apparent inconsistencies cannot be resolved.

Other scholars say that what is meant by the implicit verses are the letters found at the beginning of certain chapters. (These are known as the *muqatta`ah*-letters, like *Alif, Lam, Mim, Alif, Lam Ra', Ha, Mim*, whose real meaning is unknown).

We must, however, remember that the implicit verses are so-called when read in relation to the explicit verses. This denotes that, accompanying the hidden meaning of the implicit, there is a surface (or literal) meaning whereby the real and the apparent meanings come together in intricate relationship with one another.

It should be understood that the letters at the opening of certain chapters do not have any literal meaning. It seems that a group of misguided men use the implicit verses to mislead people, but never in Islam has one heard of anyone trying to use the *muqatta`ah*-letters to do so.

Some commentators say that the meaning of the word *mutashabih*, (in the verse), refers to the famous story[8] of the Jews who wanted to find an indication of the duration of Islam within the order of the letters, but the Prophet used

---

8. Al-`Ayyashi, *Kitab al-tafsir*, vol. 1, p. 16; al-Qummi, *Tafsir*, beginning of the commentary on *Surat al-Baqarah*; al-Huwayzi, *Tafsir nur al-thaqalayn*, vol. 1, p. 22.

to read the letters one after the other and so confuse their calculations.

This view is also without substance since, even if the story is true, it is neither of sufficient impact nor conviction to be considered as an interpretation of the implicit verses. Whatever the Jews talked, it contained no malice because, even if the religion, *deen*, of Islam was for a limited period of time (and, thus, subject to abrogation), their remarks would in no way be a criticism of the purity and reality of Islam considering that all religions revealed by God prior to Islam were for a specific period and open to abrogation.

Secondly, this view implies that the word *ta'wil* (which may be translated as "interpretation") in the verse refers to a meaning other than the apparent literal meaning and that it is used only as a reference to the implicit verses. This is incorrect, as we shall see in a later chapter dealing with exegesis *ta'wil*, and revelation, *tanzil* (the actual text or letter of the verse) how exegesis in Qur'anic terminology does not refer to one meaning but to several, encompassing such terms as realization, fulfillment, interpretation and explanation.

We shall also discuss how all Qur'anic verses have a specific interpretation, *ta'wil* and not just their explicit and implicit definitions. On examination, the words of the explicit verses (*ayat muhkamah*), are seen to describe the phrase "They are the source of the Book," meaning that the explicit verses include the most important subjects of the Book, and the theme of the rest of the verses is secondary and dependent upon them.

This implies that the real point intended to be conveyed by the implicit verses refers back to the explicit verses. Thus, the meanings of the implicit are illuminated by referring back to the source (or explicit) verses.

Thus we are left with no verses which have no obvious indication as to their true meaning; they are either immediately clear by virtue of their being in the class of explicit verses or, in the case of the implicit, made clear by the other explicit verses. As for the *muqatta'ah*-letters at the beginning of the *chapters*, they do not have any apparent meaning since they are not words in the normal sense and possess no meaning comprehensible to man; thus, they are outside of the classification of explicit and implicit.

Again, we would refer the reader to an examination of the following verse in order to emphasize the truth of our view: *"And so why do they not reflect upon the Qur'an or are there locks upon their hearts."* [47:24] And, likewise, the verse, *"and why do they not reflect upon the Qur'an, if it were from other than God they would have found much inconsistency in it."* [4:82]

The Commentary of the Imams of the Prophet's Family Concerning the Explicit and the Implicit Verses

It is made clear from the different commentaries of the Imams that there is always a way to discover the real meaning and aim of the implicit verses. Each verse, even if its meaning is not apparent, can be explained by reference to other verses. Thus the real meaning of the implicit verses can be found in relation to the explicit verses.

For instance, the verse *"The Beneficent, One who is established on the throne,"* [20:5] and again the verse, *"And your*

Lord came," [89:22] appear to ascribe bodily characteristics to God, but when compared with the verse, *"Nothing is as His likeness,"* [42:11] it becomes clear that the "sitting" on the throne or the "coming" of God has a meaning other than a physical one. The Prophet, describing the Qur'an, says:

> *In truth the Qur'an was not revealed so that one part may contradict the other but rather was revealed so that one part may verify the other. So that what you understand of it then act accordingly and that which is unclear for you then simply believe in it[9].*

The Commander of the Faithful, `Ali, said that one part of the Qur'an bears witness to another and one part clarifies the other[10]. The sixth Imam said the explicit verse is that which one acts in accordance with, and the implicit is that which is unclear only for the man who is ignorant of its real meaning[11].

From these narrations, we may conclude that the question of explicit and implicit is relative; it is possible that a verse may seem explicit to one person and implicit to another. It is said of the eighth Imam that he considered, *"the person who refers to the implicit* mutashabih, *verses in the Qur'an to the corresponding clarifying explicit verses,"* as having *"found guidance to the right path."*

He is also reported to have said that,

> *In truth in our traditions are recorded implicit verses like the explicit of the Qur'an, so refer the implicit to*

---

9. Al-`Amili, *al-Durr al-manthur*, vol. 2, p. 8.

10. Al-Sharif al-Radi, *Nahj al-balaghah*, Discourse no. 131.

11. Al-`Ayyashi, op. cit., vol. 1, p. 162.

> *its corresponding explicit verse, or tradition, and do not follow the implicit and go astray*[12].

Thus it is clear from the traditions and, in particular, the last tradition, that the implicit verse is one which does not contain a clear meaning without reference to the explicit verse, and not that there exists no means to understand it.

The Qur'an Possesses Revelation and Exegesis

We shall discuss the word, exegesis, *ta'wil*, in relation to three Qur'anic verses. Firstly, in the verses concerning the implicit *mutashabih* and the explicit verses:

> *But those in whose hearts is doubt pursue, in truth, that which is allegorical talking dissension by seeking to explain it. None knows its explanation except God* [3:7].

Secondly, the verses,

> *In truth we have brought them a scripture which we expound with knowledge, a guidance and a mercy for a people who believe. Do they await anything but the fulfillment of it?* [7:52-53]

(Here the word *ta'wil* is used connoting the appearance or clarification of meaning).

> *On the day when the fulfillment of it comes, those who are forgetful of it will say: the messenger of our Lord brought the truth.* [7:53].

---

12. Ibn Babuyah, `Uyun akhbar al-Rida, vol. 1, p. 290.

Thirdly, the verse:

> *And this Qur'an is not such as could ever be invented ... but they denied that, the knowledge of which they could not encompass and the interpretation (ta'wil) of which had not yet come to them. Even so it was that those before them deny. Then see what was the consequence in the wrongdoers. [10:37,39].*

In conclusion, we should note that the word exegesis *ta'wil* comes from the word *awl*, meaning a return. As such, *ta'wil* indicates that particular meaning towards which the verse is directed. The meaning of revelation *tanzil*, as opposed to *ta'wil*, is clear or according to the obvious meaning of the words as they were revealed.

The Meaning of Exegesis, According to the Commentators and Scholars

There is considerable disagreement as to the meaning of exegesis, *ta'wil*, and it is possible to count more than ten different views. There are, however, two views which have gained general acceptance. The first is that of the early generation of scholars who used the word exegesis, *ta'wil*, as a synonym for commentary, or *tafsir*.

According to this view, all Qur'anic verses are open to *ta'wil* although according to the verse, *"nobody knows its interpretation (ta'wil) except God,"* it is the implicit verses whose interpretation (*ta'wil*) is known only to God. For this reason, a number of the early scholars said that the implicit verses are those with *muqatta`ah*-letters at the beginning of the chapter since they are the only verses in the Qur'an whose meaning is not known to everyone.

This interpretation has been demonstrated in the previous section as being incorrect, a view which is shared by certain of the late scholars. They argued that since there is a way of finding out the meaning of any verse, particularly since the *muqatta`ah*-letters are obviously not in the same classification as the implicit verses then the distinction between the two (*muqatta`ah* and implicit, *mutashabih*) is clear.

Secondly, the view of the later scholars is that exegesis refers to the meaning of a verse beyond its literal meaning and that not all verses have exegesis; rather only the implicit, whose ultimate meaning is known only to God. The verses in question here are those which refer to the human qualities of coming, going, sitting, satisfaction, anger and sorrow apparently attributed to God and, also, those verses which apparently ascribe faults to the messengers and Prophets of God (when in reality they are infallible).

The view that the word exegesis refers to a meaning other than the apparent one has become quite accepted. Moreover, within the divergence of opinion amongst scholars, exegesis has come to mean "to transfer" the apparent meaning of a verse to a different meaning by means of a proof called *ta'wil*; this method is not without obvious inconsistencies[13].

Although this view has gained considerable acceptance, it is incorrect and cannot be applied to the Qur'anic verses for the following reasons. Firstly, the verses,

Do they await anything but the fulfillment of it? [7:53]

---

13. Since explaining the meaning of exegesis (*ta'wil*), and at the same time, recognizing that no one but God knows that *ta'wil* meaning is self-contradictory, the scholars in question have put forward this view as a hypothesis rather than as a truth.

and,

> *but they denied that, the knowledge of which they could not encompass and the interpretation of which had not yet come to them. [10:39]*

indicate that the whole Qur'an has exegesis, not just the implicit verses as claimed by this group of scholars.

Secondly, implied in this view is that there are Qur'anic verses whose real meaning is ambiguous and hidden from the people, only God knowing their real meaning. However, a book which declares itself as challenging and excelling in its linguistic brilliance could hardly be described as eloquent if it failed to transmit the meaning of its own words.

Thirdly, if we accept this view, then the validity of the Qur'an comes under question since, according to the verse,

> *Why do they not reflect upon the Qur'an, if it were from other than God they would have found in it many inconsistencies. [4:82]*

one of the proofs that the Qur'an is not the speech of man is that, despite having been revealed in widely varying and difficult circumstances, there is no inconsistency in it, neither in its literal meaning nor in its inner meaning, and any initial inconsistency disappears upon reflection.

If it is believed that a number of the implicit verses disagree with the sound, or *muhkam*, or explicit, verses this disagreement may be resolved by explaining that what is intended is not the literal meaning but rather another meaning known only to God. However, this explanation will never prove that the Qur'an is "not the speech of man." If by exegesis we change any inconsistency in the explicit, or sound (*muhkam*), verses to another meaning beyond the literal, it is clear that we may also do this for the speech and writing of man.

Fourthly, there is no proof that exegesis indicates a meaning other than the literal one and that, in the Qur'anic verses which mention the word exegesis, the literal meaning is not intended.

On three occasions in the story of Joseph, the interpretation of his dream[14] is called *ta'wil* (exegesis). It is clear that the interpretation of a dream is not fundamentally different from the actual appearance of the dream; rather, it is the interpretation of what is portrayed in a particular form in the dream. Thus Joseph saw his father, mother and brother falling to the ground in the form of the sun, the moon and the stars.

Likewise, the king of Egypt saw the seven-year drought in the form of seven lean cows eating the seven fat cows and also, the seven green ears of corn and the seven dry ears. Similarly, the dreams of Joseph's two fellow-inmates in the prison; one saw himself pouring wine for the king (in the form of the first pressing of wine), while the second saw himself crucified (in the form of birds eating from the bread basket on his head).

The dream of the king of Egypt is related in the same chapter (12), verse 43 and its interpretation, from Joseph, in verses 47-49 when he says,

> ...*you will sow seven years as usual, but whatever you reap leave it in the ear, all except a little which you will eat. Then after that will come seven hard years which will devour all that you have prepared*

---

14. Joseph's dream is mentioned in the third verse of chapter 12, "Joseph", (when he says to his father in verse 4: *"O father I saw in a dream eleven stars, the Sun and the Moon making prostration to me"*) and its interpretation is related by Joseph in verse 100: *"[Joseph] placed his parents on the dais [when they arrived from Egypt after years of separation and then his parents and his brother] fell down before him prostrate and he said: O my father! This is the interpretation of my dream."*

for them, save a little of that which you have stored. Then after that will come a year when people will have plenteous crops and then they will press (meaning wine and oil).

The dream of Joseph's fellow-inmates in the prison occurs in verse 36 of the same chapter. One of the two young men says to Joseph, *"I dreamt that I was carrying upon my head bread which the birds were eating."*

The interpretation of the dream is related by Joseph in verse 41,

O my two fellow-prisoners! As for one of you he will pour out wine for his Lord to drink and as for the other, he will be crucified so that the birds will eat from his head.

In a similar fashion, God relates the story of Moses and Khidr in the chapter "The Cave" [18:71-82]. Khidr made a hole in the boat; thereafter, killed a boy and, finally, straightened a leaning wall. After each event, Moses protested and Khidr explained the meaning and reality of each action which he had carried out on the orders of God; this he referred to as *ta'wil*.

Thus it is clear that the reality of the event and the dream-picture which portrayed the event-to-be are basically the same: the *ta'wil*, or interpretation, does not have a meaning other than the apparent one.

Likewise God says, talking about weights and measures, *"Fill the measure when you measure and weigh with a right balance, that is proper and better in the end,"* (that is, more fitting in the final determination of the Day of Reckoning) [17:35].

It is clear that the word *ta'wil* used here in respect to the measuring and weighing refers to fair dealing in business practices. Thus the *ta'wil* used in this way is not different from the literal meaning of the words "measuring" and "weighing"; it merely deepens and extends the significance of the mundane to include a spiritual dimension.

This spiritual dimension is of significance for the believer who has in mind the reckoning of the final day together with his own day-to-day reckoning in the affairs of trade.

In another verse God again uses the word *ta'wil*,

> *and if you have any dispute concerning any matter, refer it to God and the messenger . . . that is better and more fitting in the end [4:59].*

It is clear that the meaning of *ta'wil* and the referring of the dispute to God and His messenger is to establish the unity of society and to show how each action or event in a community has a spiritual significance.

Thus, the *ta'wil* refers to a tangible ordinary reality and is not in opposition to the actual text in the verses which refers to the dispute.

In all, there are sixteen occasions in the Qur'an in which the word *ta'wil* is used but on no occasion does it have a meaning other than the literal text. We may say, therefore, that the word *ta'wil* is used to extend the idea expressed to include a further meaning which, (as will be made clear in the next section), is still in accordance with the actual word *ta'wil* occurring in the verse.

Thus, in the light of these examples, there is no reason why we should take the word *ta'wil* in the verse about the explicit *muhkam*, and implicit, *mutashabih*, meanings to indicate *"a meaning basically other than the apparent meaning."*

The Meaning of Exegesis in the Tradition of the Qur'anic Sciences

What is apparent from the verses in which the word *ta'wil* occurs is that *ta'wil* does not indicate a literal meaning. It is clear that the actual words of the dream described in chapter 12, "Joseph", do not in themselves contain the literal interpretation of the dream; the meaning of the dream becomes clear from the interpretation.

And, likewise, in the story of Moses and Khidr, the actual words of the story are not the same as the interpretation which Khidr gave Moses. Moreover, in the verse,

> *fill the measure when you measure and weigh with a right balance,*

the language does not in itself indicate the particular economic conditions which we are intended to understand. Again, in the verse,

> *And if you have a dispute concerning any matter then refer it to God and the messenger,*

there is no immediate literal indication that what is meant is the Unity of Islam.

Thus, although the words indicate something not essentially different from their literal meaning, there is, nevertheless, in all the verses the same shifting of perspective, namely, from the actual words to the intended meaning.

Moreover, all the meanings are based on a real situation, an actual physical event. In the case of the dream, the interpretation has an external reality which appears before its actual occurrence in a special form to the dreamer. Likewise, in the story of Moses and Khidr, the interpretation that the latter gives is, in fact, a reality which is to take place as a result of his action.

Therefore, the interpretation of the event is rooted in the event. In the verse which orders man to fair dealing and measuring, the aspect of the verse is a reality which appears as a social benefit. Thus the order is connected to the effect it is supposed to have in the raising up of society and, in particular, of trade. In the verse concerning referral of the dispute to God and His messenger, the meaning is again fixed to reality, namely, the spiritualization of the life of the community.

To conclude, we may say that interpretation of each verse springs from a reality; the interpretation looks forward to or, in a subtle way, actually brings into being the reality it is talking about. Thus its meaning both contains and springs from a future or ulterior event. Just as the interpreter makes the interpretation meaningful, so the manifestation of the interpretation is already a reality for the interpreter.

The idea is also present in the form of the Qur'an since this sacred book has as its source realities and meanings other than the material and physical or, we may say, beyond the sensory level. Thus it expresses meanings which are more expansive than those contained in the words and phrases used by man in the material world. Although these realities and meanings are not contained in the literal explanation of man, the Qur'an uses the same language to inform man of the unseen and to produce correct belief and good action.

Thus, through belief in the unseen, in the last day and in the meeting with God, man adopts a system of morals and a quality of character which allows him to achieve happiness and well-being. In this way the Qur'an produces a spiritual effect which, in turn, produces a physical social change, the importance of which will become clear on the Day of Resurrection and the meeting with God.

There is further reference to this same theme when God says in chapter 43:2-4,

> *By the Book which makes plain. Take heed, we have appointed it a lecture in Arabic that perhaps you will understand. And indeed the source of the Book which we possess, it is indeed sublime, decisive.*

It is sublime, in that the ordinary understanding cannot fully comprehend it, and decisive in that it cannot be faulted.

The relationship of the last part of the verse to the meaning of exegesis *ta'wil*, (as we have discussed above) is clear. It says, in particular, that *"perhaps you will understand,"* implying that one may or may not understand it; it does not imply that one will understand the book fully, merely by studying it.

As we have seen in the verse concerning the explicit *muhkam*, and the implicit *mutashabih*, knowledge of exegesis *ta'wil*, is particular to God; moreover, when in this same verse corrupt men are blamed for following the implicit *mutashabih*, verses and for intending to sow dissension and conflict by searching for an exegesis, *ta'wil*, or special interpretation, it does not state that they necessarily find it.

The exegesis of the Qur'an is a reality, or several realities, which are to be found in the Source Book, the Book of Decrees with God; the Source Book is part of the unseen and far from the reach of corrupters. The same idea is treated again in chapter 56:75-80 when God says,

> *Indeed I swear by the places of the Stars – And truly that is surely a tremendous oath if you but knew – that*

> *this is indeed a noble Qur'an, in a book kept hidden, which none touch except the purified, a revelation from the Lord of the Worlds.*

It is clear that these verses establish for the Qur'an two aspects, namely the position of the hidden book protected from being touched and the aspect of revelation which is understandable by the people. What is of particular interest to us in this verse is the phrase of exception, *"except the purified."* According to this phrase, we can arrive at an understanding of the reality of the exegesis of the Qur'an.

This positive view of man's capability to understand the Qur'an does not conflict with the negation of the verse, *"And no one knows its ta'wil except God."* Since the comparison of the two verses produces a whole which is independent and harmonious. Thus we understand that God is alone in understanding these realities, yet one may come to know these truths by His leave and teaching.

Knowledge of the unseen is, according to many verses, the special domain of God but in chapter 72:26-27, those who are worthy are excepted from this: *"He is the knower of the unseen and He reveals to no one His secret, except to every messenger whom He has chosen."* Again we conclude that knowledge of the unseen is particular to God and that it is fitting for no one except Him and for those he gives leave to.

Thus the purified amongst men take the verse concerning the "purified ones" as leave to enter into contact with the reality of the Qur'an. In a similar way we read in chapter 33:33, *"God's wish is but to remove uncleanliness from you, O people of the Household, and clean you with a thorough cleaning."* This verse was revealed, (according to a sound tradition with an unbroken chain of transmission), specifically with regard to the family of the Prophet.

The Existence of Abrogating and Abrogated Verses in the Qur'an

Among the verses in the Qur'an containing orders or laws, there are verses that abrogate verses previously revealed and acted upon. These abrogating verses are called *nasikh* and those whose validity they terminate are called *mansukh*.

For example, at the beginning of the Prophet's mission, Muslims were ordered to cultivate peace and friendship with the people of the Book, *"Forgive and be indulgent (towards them) until God gives command,"* [2:109]. Some time later, fighting was allowed and the order to establish peace was abrogated:

> *Fight against such as those who have been given the Book but who believe not in God nor the last day, and do not forbid that which God has forbidden by His messenger, and follow not the religion of truth... [9:29].*

The common notion of abrogation, that is, a cancelling of one law or code by another, is based on the idea that a new law is needed because of a mistake or shortcoming in the previous one. It is clearly inappropriate to ascribe a mistake in law-making to God, Who is perfect, and whose creation admits of no flaws.

However, in the Qur'an, the abrogating verses mark the end of the validity of the abrogated verses because their heed and effect was of a temporary or limited nature. In time the new law appears and announces the end of the validity of the earlier law. Considering that the Qur'an was revealed over a period of twenty-three years in ever-changing circumstances, it is not difficult to imagine the necessity of such laws.

It is in this light that we should regard the wisdom of abrogation within the Qur'an:

> *And when we put a revelation in place of (another) revelation and God knows best what He reveals – they say: you are just inventing it. Most of them do not know. Say: The Holy Spirit (Gabriel) has revealed it from your hand with truth and as a guidance and good news for those who have surrendered (to God) [16:101-102].*

Applicability and Validity of the Qur'an

Bearing in mind that the Qur'an is valid for all times, the verses revealed in special circumstances informing Muslims of their specific duties are also valid for those who, in future, experience the same circumstances. Similarly, those verses which praise or reproach certain qualities, and promise reward or threaten punishment accordingly, are applicable to all ages and places. Thus the meaning of a verse is not limited to the circumstances or the times of its revelation.

Similar circumstances occurring subsequent to the revelation of a verse are to be followed; this is known in Qur'anic Science as *jary*, or applicability. The fifth Imam said, *"were a verse after its revelation to pass away with the passing away of that people, then nothing would have remained of the Qur'an."* As long as the heavens and the earth exist, there are verses for every people, wherever they be, which they may read and act upon for the benefit or reject at their loss[15].

---

15. Al-`Ayyashi, op. cit., vol. 1, p. 10.

Qur'anic Commentary: Its Advent and Development

Commentary on the words and expressions used in the Qur'an began at the time of the first revelation. The Prophet himself undertook the teaching of the Qur'an and the explanation of its meanings and intent.

Thus in chapter 16:44 God says, *"And we have revealed to you the Remembrance that you may explain to mankind that which has been revealed for them."* And He says in 62:2, *"He it is Who has sent among the unlettered ones a messenger of their own, to recite to them His revelations and to make them grow and to teach them the Scripture and wisdom."*

At the time of the Prophet a group of men, on his orders, were instructed to read, record and learn the Qur'an by heart. When the Prophet's companions passed away, other Muslims took over the responsibility of learning and teaching the Qur'an; and so it has continued until the present day.

The Science of Qur'anic Commentary and the Different Groups of Commentators

After the death of the Prophet a group of his companions, including Ubayy ibn Ka`b, `Abd Allah ibn Mas`ud, Jabir ibn `Abd Allah al-Ansari, Abu Sa`id al-Khudri, `Abd Allah ibn al-Zubayr, `Abd Allah ibn `Umar, Anas, Abu Hurayrah, Abu Musa, and, above all, the famous `Abd Allah ibn `Abbas, were occupied with the Science of Commentary. Just as they had heard the Prophet explaining the meanings of the verses, they would transmit it orally to other trustworthy persons.

The traditions specifically concerned with the subject of Qur'anic verses number over two hundred and forty; many were transmitted through weak chains of transmission and the texts of some have been rejected as incorrect or forged. Sometimes the transmission would include commentaries based on personal judgments rather than on a narration of the actual sayings, *hadiths*, from the Prophet.

The later Sunni commentators considered this kind of commentary as part of the body of Sayings of The Prophet, since the companions were learned in the science of Qur'anic commentary. They argued that these companions had acquired their knowledge of this science from the Prophet himself and that it was unlikely they would say anything which they themselves had invented.

There is, however, no absolute proof for their reasoning. A large proportion of these sayings, or traditions, about the reasons and historical circumstances of the revelation of verses do not possess an acceptable chain of narration. It should be noted that many of the narrators like Ka`b al-Akhbar, were learned companions who had belonged to the Jewish faith before accepting Islam.

Moreover, it should not be overlooked that Ibn `Abbas usually expressed the meanings of verses in poetry. In one of his narrations over two hundred questions of Nafi` ibn al-Azraq are replied to in the form of poetry; al-Suyuti in his book, *al-Itqan*, related one hundred and ninety of these questions.

It is evident, therefore, that many of the narrations made by the commentators amongst the companions cannot be counted as actual narrations from the Prophet himself; therefore, such additional material related by the companions must be rejected.

The second group of commentators were the companions of the followers (*tabi`un*), who were the students of the companions. Amongst them we find Mujahid, Sa`id ibn Jubayr, `Ikrimah and Dahhak. Also from this group were Hasan al-Basri, `Ata' ibn Abi Rabah, `Ata' ibn Abi Muslim, Abu al-`Aliyah, Muhammad ibn Ka`b al-Qurazi, Qatadah, `Atiyah, Zayd ibn Aslam, Ta'us al-Yamani[16].

The third group were comprised of the students of the second group, namely, Rabi` ibn Anas, `Abd al-Rahman ibn Zayd ibn Aslam, Abu Salih al-Kalbi and others[17]. The *tabi`un* sometimes narrated the commentary on a verse as a tradition of the Prophet or of the companions and, sometimes, they explained its meaning without attributing a narrator to the source, this they did especially when there was any doubt as to the identity of the narrator. The later commentators treat these narrations as traditions of the Prophet, but count them as *mawquf* in their science of the levels of *hadiths* (that is as a tradition whose chain of narration does not reach back to the Prophet).

The fourth group comprised the first compilers of commentaries, like Sufyan ibn `Uyaynah[18], Waki` ibn al-Jarrah, Shu`bah al-Hajjaj and `Abd ibn Humayd; others

---

16. Mujahid, a famous commentator, died 100 or 103 A.H. (al-Nawawi, *Tahdhib al-asma'*). Sa`id ibn Jubayr, a pupil of Ibn `Abbas, was martyred at the hands of al-Hajjaj in 94 A.H. (*Tahdhib*). `Ikrimah, a pupil of Sa`id ibn Jubayr, died 104 A.H. (*Tahdhib*). Dahhak was a pupil of `Ikrimah (Ibn Hajar al-`Asqalani, *Lisan al-mizan*). Hasan al-Basri, an ascetic and commentator died in 110 A.H. (*Tahdhib*). `Ata' ibn Abi Muslim was a pupil of Ibn Jubayr and `Ikrimah and died in 133 A.H. (*Tahdhib*). `Ata' ibn Abi Rabah, a commentator and jurisprudent, a pupil of Ibn `Abbas, died 115 A.H. (*Tahdhib*). Muhammad ibn Ka`b al-Qarthi, a well known commentator, was a descendant of a Jewish tribe Banu Qurayzah (*Tahdhib*). Qatadah, one of the greatest commentators, was a pupil of Hasan al-Basri and `Ikrimah, and died in 117 A.H. (*Tahdhib*). `Atiyah was a *rawi* (transmitter) of Ibn `Abbas (*Lisan*). Zayd ibn Aslam, a freed slave of `Umar ibn al-Khattab, died 136 A.H. (*Tahdhib*). Ta`us al-Yamani, a great scholar of his time, a pupil of Ibn `Abbas, died 106 A.H. (*Tahdhib*).

17. `Abd al-Rahman ibn Zayd, son of Zayd ibn Aslam, is regarded as a commentator. Abu Salih al-Kalbi, a genealogist and commentator, lived in the second century A.H.

18. Sufyan ibn `Uyaynah of Mecca, belongs to the second group of *tabi`un*, died 198 A.H. (*Tahdhib*). Waki` ibn al-Jarrah of Kufa, like Sufyan belongs to the second group, died 197 A.H. (*Tahdhib*). To the same group also belongs `Abd ibn Humayd, died in 160 A.H. (*Tahdhib*).

from this group include Ibn Jarir al-Tabari, the author of the famous Qur'anic Commentary[19].

This group recorded the sayings of the companions and the followers of the companions with a chain of narrators in their works of commentary; they avoided expressing personal opinions except, perhaps, Ibn Jarir al-Tabari who sometimes expressed his views by indicating his preference when discussing two similar traditions. The basis of the work of later groups may be traced to this group.

The fifth group omitted the chain of narrators in their writings and contented themselves with a simple relation of the text of the traditions. Some scholars regard these commentators as the source of varying views in the commentaries by connecting many traditions to a companion or a follower without verifying their validity or mentioning their chain of narration. Consequently, confusion has arisen allowing many false traditions to enter the body of traditions, thus undermining the reputation of this section of *hadith* literature.

Careful examination of the chains of transmission of the traditions leaves one in doubt as to the extent of the deceitful additions and false testimonies. Many conflicting traditions can be traced to one companion or follower and many traditions, which are complete fabrications, may be found amongst this body of narrations.

Thus reasons for the revelation of a particular verse, including the abrogating and abrogated verses, do not seem to accord with the actual order of the verses. No more than one or two of the traditions are found to be acceptable when submitted to such an examination.

---

19. Muhammad ibn Jarir al-Tabari (died 310 A.H.) was one of the great Sunni scholars (*Lisan*).

It is for this reason that Imam Ahmad ibn Hanbal, who himself was born before this generation of narrators, said, *"Three things have no sound base: military virtues, bloody battles and the traditions pertaining to Qur'anic commentary,"* Imam al-Shafi`i relates that only about one hundred traditions from Ibn `Abbas have been confirmed as valid.

The sixth group consists of those commentators who appeared after the growth and development of the various Islamic Sciences and each undertook the study of Qur'anic commentary according to his specialization: al-Zajjaj studied the subject from the grammatical point of view; al-Wahidi and Abu Hayyan[20] investigated the verses by studying the inflection of the verbs, the vowels and the diacritical points.

There is also commentary on the rhetoric and eloquence of the verses by al-Zamakhshari[21] in his work entitled *al-Kashshaf*. There is a theological discussion in the "Grand Commentary" of Fakhr al-Din al-Razi[22]. The gnosis of Ibn al-`Arabi and `Abd al-Razzaq al-Kashani[23] treated in their commentaries. Other narrators, like al-Tha`labi, record the history of transmission of the traditions[24]. Some commentators, among them al-Qurtubi[25], concentrate on aspects of *fiqh* (jurisprudence).

There also exists a number-of commentaries composed of many of these sciences, such as *Ruh al-bayan* by Shaykh

---

20. Al-Zajjaj, a grammarian, died 310 A.H. (al-Tabrizi, *Rayhanat al-adab*). Al-Wahidi, a grammarian and commentator, died 468 A.H. (*Rayhanah*). Abu Hayyan al-Andalusi, a grammarian, commentator and reciter of the Our'an, died in Cairo 745 A.H. (*Rayhanah*).

21. Al-Zamakhshari, the author of *al-Kashshaf*, died in 538 A.H. (Hajji Khalifah, *Kashf al-Zunun*).

22. Fakhr al-Din al-Razi, a theologian and commentator, the author of a *tafsir* entitled *Mafatih al-ghayb*, died 606 A.H. (*Kashf al-Zunun*).

23. `Abd al-Razzaq al-Kashani, a famous Sufi, died 720 or 751 A.H. (*Rayhanah*)

24. Ahmad ibn Muhammad al-Tha`labi, the author of a well known commentary (*tafsir*) on the Qur'an, died 426 or 427 A.H. (*Rayhanah*).

25. Muhammad ibn Ahmad ibn Abi Bakr al-Qurtubi died in 668 A.H. (*Rayhanah*).

Isma`il Haqqi[26], *Ruh al-Ma`ani* by Shihab al Din Mahmud al-Alusi al-Baghdadi[27] *Ghara'ib al-Qur'an* by Nizam al-Din al-Nisaburi[28]. This group rendered a great service to the Science of Qur'anic commentary in that it brought the Science out of a state of stagnation (characteristic of the fifth group before it), and developed it into a Science of precise investigation and theory.

However, if one were to examine closely the precision of this group's research, one would see that much of its Qur'anic commentary imposes its theories onto the Qur'an rather than allowing the content of the verses to speak for themselves.

The Methods Used by the Shi`ite Commentators and Their Different Groupings

All the groups mentioned above are Sunni commentators. Their method, used in the earliest commentaries of this period, was based on *ijtihad*, that is, the reports of the companions and the followers of the companions were examined according to certain rules in order to reach an acceptable understanding of the text. This resulted in varying opinions amongst those making *ijtihad* and caused disorder, contradiction and, even, fabrication to enter into the body of the traditions.

The method employed by the Shi`ite commentators, however, was different, with the result that the patterning of

---

26. Written by Isma`il Haqqi (died 1137 A.H., *Dhayl Kashf al-Zunun*).

27. Written by Shihab al-Din Mahmud al-Alusi (died 1270 A.H., *Dhayl Kashf al-Zunun*).

28. Al-Nisaburi died 728 A.H. (*Dhayl Kashf al-Zunun*).

the groups was also different. The Shi`ite commentators in their study of a verse of the Qur'an, viewed the explanation given by the Prophet as proof of the meaning of the verse, they did not accept the saying of the companions, or the followers, as indisputable proof that the tradition was from the Prophet.

The Shi`ite commentators only recognized as valid an unbroken chain of narration from the Prophet and through members of his family. Accordingly, in using and transmitting the verses concerning Qur'anic commentary, they restricted themselves to the use of traditions transmitted by the Prophet and by the Imams of the Prophet's family. This has given rise to the following groups:

The first group comprises those who have learned these traditions from the Prophet and from the Imams of the Prophet's family, studying and recording them according to their own method but not in any particular order. Among them we may mention such scholars as Zararah, Muhammad ibn Muslim, Ma`ruf and Jarir who were companions of the fifth and sixth Imams[29].

The second group comprises the first compilers of the commentaries, like Furat ibn Ibrahim al-Kufi, Abu Hamzah al-Thumali, Muhammad al-`Ayyashi, `Ali ibn Ibrahim al-Qummi and al-Nu`mani who lived between the second and fourth centuries after *Hijrah*[30]. The method of this group was similar to that of the fourth Sunni group of Commentators.

---

29. Zararah ibn A`yun and Muhammad ibn Muslim were special companions of Imam Baqir and Imam Sadiq. Ma`ruf ibn Kharbudh as well as Jarir were special companions of Imam Sadiq.

30. Furat ibn Ibrahim al-Kufi, known for his commentary on the Qur'an, was one of the teachers of `Ali ibn Ibrahim al-Qummi (*Rayhanah*). Abu Hamzah al-Thumali was a special companion of Imam Sajjad and Imam Baqir (*Rayhanah*). Muhammad ibn Mas`ud al-`Ayyashi al-Kufi al-Samarqandi was one of the great Shi`ite scholars who lived in the second half of the third century A.H. (*Rayhanah*). `Ali ibn Ibrahim al-Qummi, who lived at the end of the third and the beginning of the fourth century A.H., was one of the great teachers of Shi`ite tradition. Muhammad ibn Ibrahim al-Nu`mani, a student of al-Kulayni, lived at the beginning of the fourth century A.H. (*Rayhanah*).

Thus, they avoided any kind of *ijtihad* or passing of judgment. We should remember that the Imams of the Prophet's family were living amongst Muslims and available for questioning (on matters of commentary, for example) for a period of almost three hundred years. Thus the first groups were not divided chronologically but rather according to their relationship with the Imams.

There are very few who recorded the tradition without a chain of transmission. As an example, we should mention one of the students of al-`Ayyashi who omitted to record the chains of transmission. It was his work, instead of the original of al-`Ayyashi which came into common use.

The third group comprises masters of various sciences, like al-Sharif al-Radi[31] who provided a commentary concerned with Qur'anic language and Shaykh al-Tusi who wrote a commentary and analysis on metaphysical matters[32]. Included, too, is Sadr al-Din al-Shirazi's philosophic work[33], al-Maybudi al-Kunabadi's gnostic commentary[34] and `Abd `Ali al-Huwayzi's commentary *Nur al-Thaqalayn*[35]. Hashim al-Bahrani composed the commentary *al-Burhan*[36] and al-Fayd al-Kashani compiled the work known as *al-Safi*[37].

---

31. Muhammad ibn al-Husayn al-Musawi al-Sharif al-Radi (died in 404 or 406 A.H.), a great Shi`ite scholar, known for his compilation *Nahj al-Balaghah* (*Rayhanah*).

32. Shaykh al-Ta'ifah Muhammad ibn al-Hasan al-Tusi, the author of *al-Tahdhib* and *al-Istibsar*, the well known canonical books of the Shi`ite. He died in 460 A.H. (*Rayhanah*).

33. Sadr al-Din Muhammad ibn Ibrahim al-Shirazi, a famous philosopher, the author of *Asrar al-ayat* and *Majmu`at al-tafasir*, died in 1050 A.H. (Muhammad Baqir al-Khwansari, *Rawdat al-Jannat*, vol. 4, pp. 120-122).

34. Rashid al-Din Ahmad ibn Muhammad al-Maybudi, the author of *Kashf al-Asrar*, lived in the sixth century A.H.

35. `Abd `Ali al-Huwayzi al-Shirazi died in 1112 A.H. (*Rayhanah*).

36. Hashim al-Bahrani died in 1107 A.H. (*Rayhanah*).

37. Muhammad Muhsin ibn al-Murtada al-Fayd al-Kashani, the author of *al-Safi* and *al-Asfa*, died in 1091 A.H. (*Rayhanah*).

There were others who brought together many different themes to their commentaries, like Shaykh al-Tabarsi who in his *Majma` al-Bayan*[38] researches different fields of language, grammar, Qur'an recitation, gnosis of death, after-life and paradise, and knowledge of the traditions.

How Does the Qur'an Lend Itself to Interpretation?

The answer to this question is contained in the previous section where we discussed the eternal validity of the Qur'an: it speaks to, instructs and guides man now as it did in the past. As we have seen, the whole text of the Qur'an is a challenge to mankind and particularly to the enemies of Islam in that the Qur'an itself is proof of its own argument; it announces itself as a light, an illumination and an explanation of all things.

Thus a document which states and demonstrates that it is self-illuminating, hardly needs others to illuminate it. As proof that it is not the speech of man, the Qur'an says that it is a harmonious speech, without the slightest inconsistency and any seeming inconsistency may be removed through reflection on the Qur'an itself. If it were not the word of God, the Qur'an would not be as clear as it is.

Moreover, if such speech needed something or someone else to explain its meaning and purpose, it would neither be the proof nor the absolute authority that it is so obviously is. This clarity is absolute, even if a seemingly contradictory passage becomes the object of dispute; it could be understood by cross-reference to the text of the Qur'an.

---

38. Al-Fadl ibn al-Hasan al-Tabarsi died in 548 A.H. (*Rayhanah*).

For instance, at the time of the Prophet, such matters could be referred to him since his knowledge of the Qur'an was perfect and he did not need to refer to other verses for clarification. Those who insisted on disagreeing, or disbelieving in the Prophet's infallibility, were not satisfied.

Therefore, commentaries which solve problems of interpretation by quoting the commentaries of the Prophet, without giving proofs from other Qur'anic verses, are useful only for those who disbelieve in Prophethood and the Prophet's infallibility. These people do not go unmentioned in the Qur'an; we are familiar with the following verse,

> *if it had been from other than God then they would have found many inconsistencies in it. [4:82]*

This is a clear argument against those who would seek for inconsistencies in the Qur'an and find fault with the Prophet.

The Qur'an itself declares that the commentary and explanation of the Prophet is valid while the Prophet himself has confirmed the validity of the Qur'anic commentary of the Imams. We may summarize this by saying that in the Qur'an some verses may be explained by comparison with other verses and some by using the instructions and teachings of the Prophet and the Imams. The latter commentaries are not, of course, different from the explanation which is produced by comparing and analyzing different verses.

Conclusion

There are three roads open to us when making commentary upon the Qur'an. Firstly, by using knowledge that one already possesses.

Secondly, with the help of the sayings of the Prophet or Imams.

Thirdly, by using a combination of methods: by reflection and analysis, or by allowing the verse to become clarified by comparing it to other verses, or by use of the sayings of the Prophet and the Imams, whenever possible.

The third way is the one which we have outlined in the last section and it is this way which the Prophet himself and the Imams of his family indicate in their teachings[39]. As we have seen, the Prophet said that, *"The verses were revealed to confirm each other,"* and Imam `Ali said that *"One part of the Qur'an explains another and one part witnesses to the other."*

It is, moreover, clear that this method of commentary is other than that warned against by the Prophet when he said, *"Whoever makes a commentary upon the Qur'an according to his own opinion prepares for himself a place in the Fire[40]."* This method uses the Qur'an to explain itself and is not based merely on explanation arising from whim or fancy.

The first method is unacceptable and exemplifies commentary based on opinion, except in cases where it agrees with the third method. The second method is the one used by the early scholars and for many centuries afterwards, and is still in use amongst both Sunni and Shi`ite scholars of the traditions of the Prophet. This method is limited, considering the vast nature of the subject and the countless

---

39. See the beginning of al-`Ayyashi's, *Kitab al-Tafsir*, al-Fayd al-Kashani's *al-Safi*, al-Bahrani's *al-Burhan* and al-Majlisi's *Bihar al-Anwar*.

40. Al-Majlisi, ibid., vol. 1, p. 137 (chapter on *Ikhtilaf al-Akhbar*).

number of questions, (both general and particular), arising from over six thousand verses.

Where, one asks, is the answer to such questions? Where is the solution to so many intricate and perplexing questions? Or, should we refer to the body of tradition concerning the verses?

Let us not forget that the total number of traditions of the Prophet accepted and transmitted by the Sunni scholars number no more than two hundred and fifty[41]; we should also remember that many of them are weak and some even totally unacceptable. It is true that the traditions of the Prophet and the Imams transmitted by the Shi`ite scholars number a thousand and that amongst them are to be found a considerable number which are fully trustworthy.

Consideration of these traditions is not enough, however, given the countless questions which arise and the many Qur'anic verses that are not even mentioned in this body of traditions. Should one refer in such matters to the appropriate verses?

As we have explained, this is not acceptable according to the method under consideration here. Should one simply abstain from investigation and imagine that the need for knowledge is non-existent? In this case, what is one to understand by the verse,

> *And we reveal the Book to you as an exposition of all things, [16:89].*

which is clear proof that the Qur'an itself is not a mystery but rather explains, among other things, *itself*, by its own light.

---

41. Publisher's Note: We believe that `Allamah Sayyid M.H. Tabataba`i is here referring to those Sunni traditions of the Prophet that comment on Qur'anic verses.

Chapters 4:82 and 47:24 contain the injunction, *"Will they not ponder on the Qur'an."* Similarly, in chapter 38:29 *"(This book) is a Book that we have revealed to you, full of blessing, that you may ponder its revelation and those of understanding may reflect."* Likewise in Chapter 23:68, *"Have they not pondered the word, or has something come to them which did not come to their forefathers."*

What are we intended to understand by these verses? How are we to act in the light of the totally trustworthy traditions of the Prophet and the Imams in which they advise us to refer to the Qur'an itself in case of problems of interpretation and discordance of opinion? According to many well known traditions of the Prophet, transmitted in unbroken chains of transmission, one is obliged to refer the tradition to the Book of God; if the tradition is in accordance with the Book, then it is accepted and used in commentary and, if in disagreement, it is rejected.

It is clear that the meaning of these traditions is applicable when one discovers through the Science of Commentary that the inner meaning of one verse is contrary to what is contained in another verse. In this case, one must reject what one has discovered through the study of commentaries.

These traditions are the best proof that the Qur'an, like speech or writing in general, has meaning and will always have meaning, even when studied independently of the traditions. Thus it is the duty of the commentators to take into account and reflect upon the traditions of the Prophet and Imams concerning Qur'anic verses but only use those traditions which are in accordance with the verse under scrutiny.

An Example of Commentary on the Qur'an with the Aid of the Qur'an

On four occasions in the Qur'an God says *"Allah is the creator of all beings,"* [39:62]. The meaning is clear on each occasion; God is stating that everything man may possibly imagine in the world has been created by Him and is sustained by Him. However, one should not ignore the fact that in hundreds of verses the Qur'an affirms the existence of cause and effect and attributes the action of every doer to the immediate cause.

Thus the effect of the burning of fire is a direct result of the fire itself, the growing of plants, the action of the plants, the falling rain caused by the state of the sky; the actions which man chooses to undertake are, according to the Qur'an, the result (and consequent responsibility) of man. We may also say that the doer of any action is the one responsible for that action, but God is the giver of existence, the Creator of deeds and the owner of deeds.

Keeping in mind this general relationship between the Creator and His creation, we may read in chapter 32:7 *"Who made all things beautiful and good which We created."* When we join this verse to the previous one we see that beauty and goodness necessarily accompany His creation and so anything which has existence in the cosmos is also good and beautiful.

We should not forget, however, that in many verses, the Qur'an affirms the existence of good and its opposite, evil, useful things and harmful things, beauty and ugliness; and it enumerates many bad actions, wrong doers and bad events.

These are all, however, negative aspects of the human character and are mentioned as a measure of man; they are relative and not intended as proof that the creation of man is basically bad. For example, the snake or the serpent is harmful but only to man and animals who suffer the effects of its sting; to stones and earth it is harmless. Bitter taste and foul smell are unpleasant, but only to the human sense of taste and smell, not to all animals. Certain behavior may at times appear wrong but this is often the result of observing human behavior in relation to one particular society of humans; in another society or circumstance it may not be considered wrong.

Indeed, if we dispense for a moment with those negative aspects of man's character which are secondary or relative to the miracle and perfection of His creation, we witness only the beautiful symmetry and proportion of the cosmos in its entirety and the amazing beneficence of the Creator. Words are not able to describe this beauty since they themselves are part of this world of beauty.

In reality the above-mentioned verses awake man to an awareness of the relative nature of beauty and ugliness; they invite him to a comprehension of absolute beauty and prepare him for an understanding of creation as a whole. In fact, there are Qur'anic verses which explain or comment upon the different aspects of creation in the universe, either as isolated individual examples or as groupings and classes. Each creation, whether a single manifestation or joined to a larger structure and patterning, is a sign and indication of God. Whichever way we regard creation, it all points to the existence of God.

This way of understanding or seeing the universe and its signs, leads to an appreciation of the stupendous beauty which encircles the whole world and allows us to realize that it is His beauty, emanating from the domain of His power, and made visible in the signs of the skies and the earth. Each aspect of the cosmos lends beauty and dimension to everything surrounding it, yet at the same time it is insignificant in relation to the whole.

The Qur'an affirms in other verses that perfection and beauty manifest themselves from the domain of His power; thus He says in chapter 40:65 *"He is the Living One. There is no god save Him,"* and in 2:165 *". . .power belongs completely to God,"* and in 4:139, *"Truly all power belongs to God,"* and in 40:50,*"He is the knower, the All-Powerful."* On another occasion we read, in 42:11, *"And He is the Hearer, the Seer,"* and in 20:8, *"Allah! There is no god save Him. His are the most beautiful names."*

We realize from these verses that the beauty which manifests itself in the visible world has its reality in the domain of His power and grandeur. All other beauty, all other power, is illusory or metaphorical of His power.

In affirmation of this explanation, the Qur'an states that the beauty and perfection created by man is limited and temporal but that of God boundless and eternal. God emphasizes that all creation is from Him and under His power. In chapter 54:49, *"Truly we have created everything by measure"* and in the chapter 15:21, *"And there is not a thing with us but there are stores of it. And we do not send it down except in appointed measure."*

Careful observation reveals that the Book itself declares its own perfection and beauty, that it encompasses all aspects of creation and the Creator, and that there is no fault or shortcoming in it. Such is the perfection of the Qur'an, which itself is one of the signs of God, that it makes the reader forget himself in rapturous appreciation of its beauty.

This we read in 2:165 *"Those who believe are stauncher in their love of God."* Love, of its very nature, demands the self and the giving over of the self to God. It demands the handing over of one's affairs completely to Him and allowing Him to be one's Lord: *"And Allah is the protecting Friend of the believers,"* [3:68].

This idea is also contained in 2:257 which declares, *"God is the Protecting Friend of those who believe. He brings them out of darkness into light,"* and also in 6:122, *"Is he who was dead and We have raised him to life and set for him a light in which he walks among people . . ."* Likewise, we read in 58:22, *"As for such, He has written faith upon their hearts and has strengthened them with a spirit from Him."*

This spirit, this new life and light, is given by God to the person who perceives reality and truth and who understands the path of happiness and well-being in society. In another verse in 57:28, He explains the effect of such light: *"O you who believe! Be mindful of your duty to God and put faith in His messenger. He will give you twofold of His mercy and will appoint for you a light in which you shall walk."*

Again, in another verse, He makes a commentary on "faith in the Prophet" by explaining it as submission and obedience to Him; chapter 3:31, *"Say (O Muhammad, to humankind): If you love God follow me; God will love you."*

The nature of this path is explained in chapter 7:157,

> *Those who follow the messenger, the Prophet who can neither read nor write, whom they will find described in the Torah and the Gospels (which are) with them. He will enjoin on them that which is right and forbid them that which is wrong. He will make lawful for*

> *them all good things and prohibit for them only the foul; and He will relieve them of their burden and the fetters they used to wear.*

Still more vividly, the path is explained in another verse which is also a commentary on the previous verse [30:30],

> *So [Prophet] as a man of pure faith, stand firm and true in your devotion to the religion. This is the natural disposition God instilled in mankind – there is no altering God's creation – and this is the right way of life, though most people do not realize it.*

The right way of life, or *deen*, refers to the correct path for society to follow for its well-being and happiness. According to this verse, the way of Islam is also the way desired by the Creator for humankind.

In other words, the legislative framework given to man by God is the very framework which is appropriate for the creature man. This divine law is in complete harmony with the nature of man, living a life of piety and obedience.

God says in another verse [91:7-8], *"And a soul and Him who perfected it. And inspired it (with conscience of) what is wrong for it and (what is) right for it."* The Qur'an is the only revealed book which equates the happiness and well-being of man with a pure and sincere way of life.

Moreover, unlike other religions, Islam does not separate worship of God from the actual program of living; it establishes the word *deen* to mean not only religion but also life in general as well, the actual day to day routine of man, both on a personal and social level.

The Qur'an establishes a program of living which is in accord with the functioning and the reality of the cosmos, and the Qur'an mentions many of the benefits and virtues to be expected by the man of God and the lovers of Truth, including a certainty of faith and tranquility of the heart.

The Validity of the Commentary of the Prophet and the Imams

From an indication in the Qur'an itself, the commentary of the Prophet and the Imams, (as discussed in the previous sections), is established as being absolutely true. Authentication of the sayings of the Prophet and the Imams is clearly established by the existence of fully trustworthy chains of transmissions. A tradition may not, however, be recognized as totally acceptable if it has been transmitted by one chain of narration only.

The validity of the tradition may be disputed amongst the Muslim Scholars of Commentary: amongst the Sunni's a tradition of a single chain of transmission, classified in their terms as *sahih* (sound), must be accepted and acted upon; among the Shi`ite scholars a tradition with a single undisputed chain of transmission is also accepted as a proof. However, in the laws of the *shari`ah* it is not valid and must be investigated and checked before use as a proof.

Author's Note: The previous section has been specifically about the use of commentary or explanation in order to arrive at the true meaning of a verse. This includes study of the literal meanings and those hidden in metaphor. It does not include an explanation or a discussion of the linguistic and literal aspects or the science of Qur'an recitation since these do not affect the meaning.

Chapter 3
THE REVELATION OF THE QUR'AN

General Beliefs of Muslims Concerning the Revelation of the Qur'an

More than any other revealed book, especially the Torah and the New Testament, the Qur'an describes the details of the revelation, the transmittance and even accounts of the experience of the revelation. The general belief of Muslims concerning the revelation, based on the Qur'an, is that the text of the Qur'an is the actual speech of God transmitted to the Prophet by one of His chosen angels.

The name of this angel, or heavenly being, is Gabriel or the Faithful Spirit. He transmitted the word of God over a period of twenty-three years to the Prophet. He would bring the divine instructions to the Prophet, who would relate them faithfully to the people using the same words in the form of a verse.

The Prophet thus used the meaning of the verses to call the people to an understanding of faith, of belief, of social laws and of individual duties. These instructions from God to His messenger are known as the Prophecy, or the Message; the Prophet transmitted this message without making any addition to or detraction from it in any way.

The View of Contemporary Non-Muslim Writers Concerning the Revelation and Prophecy

Most contemporary writers who take an interest in different religions and ideologies adopt the following view of the Qur'an: they say the Prophet was a social genius who appeared to save society from the throes of decline into savagery and to raise it up in the cradle of civilization and freedom. They claim also that he called men to his own ideas of pure and sincere behavior by giving them a comprehensive religious form and order. They affirm that he had a pure soul and tremendous ambition; that he lived in a particularly dark and ignorant age, where only the law of force and foolish singing of verse, social chaos and selfishness, stealing, marauding and savagery were to be seen.

They describe how he was troubled by witnessing such things and, sometimes when overcome by the pain of such sights, he would withdraw from men and pass days alone in the cave in the Tihamah mountains; he would marvel at the sky and its shining stars, the earth, the mountains, the sea, the desert and all the precious means placed at the disposal of man by the Creator; he would be grieved at the bad behavior and ignorance of those around him, who had thrown away a life of well-being and happiness for a tormented succession of bestial habits.

This feeling was always present with the Prophet; he bore this pain and vexation up to his fortieth year when, according to these contemporary non-Muslim writers, he formed a plan to save his fellow-men from their miserable state of nomadic wandering, rebellious independence, selfishness and lawlessness.

This plan, called the religion of Islam, was the most suitable one for the times. The Prophet being of pure and sincere character, realized that his chaste thoughts were the Word of God and Divine Revelation which were infused in him through his virtuous nature. His good will and benevolent spirit, from which his thoughts exuded and established peace in his heart, was called the Spirit of Trustworthiness and Gabriel, the angel of revelation.

Furthermore, according to this contemporary view of Muhammad, he perceived the forces of good and happiness in nature as Angels and all the forces of bad as Satan and the *Jinn* (invisible entities). He called his own task, which he had undertaken according to his own conscience, Prophethood and himself, the deliverer of the divine message.

This explanation, however, comes from those writers who affirm the existence of God or at least some kind of nature-force, and attach a certain importance to the religion of Islam, albeit in the name of just and unbiased assessment. Those, however, who deny outright the existence of a Creator see Prophecy, revelation, divine duties, reward and punishment, the fire and the garden as mere religious politics, a lie in the name of religion to further one's own ends.

They say that the prophets were reformers who brought about social change in the name of religion. They argued that since men of past ages were drowned in ignorance and superstitious worship the prophets contained the religious order within a framework of superstitious beliefs about the origin of Creation and the day of reckoning in order to further their prospects of reform.

What the Qur'an Itself Says Concerning this Matter

Scholars who explain the power of revelation and prophecy using the above explanation, attach great importance to the Science of nature and the visible world, and claim that everything in the world works according to the laws of nature. They view historical events, right up to the present-day, as the developing and constantly changing face of nature.

Likewise, they view all revealed religions as social manifestations. Thus they would agree that if one of the geniuses of history, like Cyrus, Darius or Alexander, had announced himself as having been chosen by God as an executor of divine commands, their explanation would have been no different than that given above.

We do not intend here to establish the existence of the unseen, of the world beyond the visible world of nature; we are not saying to other scholars or scientists that any one science may only be discussed by remaining within the strict limits of that particular science. We are not suggesting that the modern sciences which investigate the properties and effects of the material world, (whether or not they be positively or negatively disposed to the creation), do not have the right to enter into an investigation of the metaphysical.

What we are saying is that any explanation they propose must be in accordance with the explanation of society, existence, nature and the cosmos given by the Qur'an. The Qur'an is an authentic document of prophecy and is the basis of all social, metaphysical and scientific discussion; the explanations of the Qur'an contain proofs against their arguments which we can enumerate and reflect upon. These proofs are connected to different Qur'anic verses discussed below.

Divine Revelation

According to the explanation of modern non-Muslims and atheists, the Prophet's nature was pure through which came to him the word of God, meaning that the divine system of thought was alive in his own thoughts; the idea of divinity manifested itself in his thoughts because he was pure and holy; it was natural (in the minds of these Scholars) for prophets to attribute these thoughts to God for, in this way, they ennobled and exalted their own task.

The Qur'an, however, strongly and convincingly denies that it is the speech or the ideas of the prophet or, indeed, of any other man. In chapters 10:38 and 11:13 the Qur'an declares that if it is the word of man then detractors of Islam should produce similar words about every subject treated in the Qur'an, namely, belief in the after-life, morals, laws, stories of past generations and other prophets, wisdom and advice. The Qur'an urges them to seek help anywhere if they do not realize that it is the word of God and not of man, but adds that even if *jinn* and man joined forces together they would not be able to produce a Qur'an like it.

In chapter 2:23 the Qur'an challenges those who consider it merely the speech of Muhammad to produce a book similar to it or even just one chapter like it. The force of this challenge becomes clear when we realize that it is issued for someone whose life should resemble that of Muhammad, namely, the life of an orphan, uneducated in any formal sense, not being able to read or write and grew up in the unenlightened age of the *jahiliyah* period (the age of ignorance) before Islam.

In 4:82 the Qur'an asks why no inconsistencies or changes appeared in the verses considering that neither the wording nor the meaning of the verses has altered despite being revealed over a period of twenty-three years. If it was the word of man and not the word of God, then it would have certainly been affected by change like all other things in the temporal world of nature and matter.

It is clear that this challenge and these explanations are not mere empty words of exultation; rather they present the Qur'an for what it is, namely the word of God.

The Qur'an establishes its own miraculous nature in hundreds of verses. This miracle is still unexplained by normal literacy standards used to "grasp" a text. Indeed successive prophets established their prophethood through similar verses revealed by God. If prophecy was merely the call of an individual conscience or the inspiration of a pure and sincere soul, then there would be no sense in claiming it as divine proof or seeking help in its miraculous nature as the Prophet, in fact, did.

Some writers interpret the many miracles of the Qur'an in terms of undisguised mockery. When we investigate the subject of their mockery we inevitably discover that the Qur'an means something other than that which they have understood.

It is not our intention to try and prove the miraculous nature of the Qur'an nor to demonstrate the soundness and authenticity of its narration; rather, we would point out that the Qur'an clearly describes the miracles of the past prophets, like Salih, Abraham, Moses and Jesus. The stories related in the Qur'an can only be understood and interpreted in the light of miraculous guidance.

Why, we may ask, if the prophets were mere men, inspired by the purity of their character, was it necessary to establish the existence of this miraculous guidance?

The Angel Gabriel

According to the explanation of the above-mentioned writers, the prophet referred to his own pure soul as the "Faithful Spirit" or the giver of revelation. The Qur'an, however, does not support this view and names Gabriel as the deliverer of the verses.

God says in chapter 2:97, *"Say (O Muhammad, to mankind): Who is an enemy to Gabriel! for it is he who has revealed (this book) to your heart by God's permission."* This verse refers to Jews who wanted to know who had revealed the Qur'an to the Prophet[42]. He replied that it was Gabriel. They said, *"We are enemies of Gabriel as he it was who gave us (the tribe of Israel) the laws and legal punishments and as we are enemies to him, we do not believe in the book which he has brought."* Thus God replies to them in the verse that Gabriel revealed the Qur'an to the Prophet by God's permission. God further says that the Qur'an is to be believed in, and that it is not the speech of Gabriel. It is important to note that the Qur'an, in the words of the above verse was revealed "to the heart" of the Prophet Muhammad by Gabriel.

In another verse [26:193-194] we read that it was transmitted by the Faithful Spirit, *"which the Faithful Spirit*

---

42. Because both verses relate the descension of the Qur'an before the Holy Prophet. It says, *"Upon their hearts"* and not "their hearts" and the heart, in the usage of the Holy Qur'an is the soul because in several places, understanding and awareness comes from the soul and is related to the heart. 26:193-195.

has brought down upon your heart." By comparison of these two verses it becomes evident that it is the angel Gabriel who is meant here by the words, "Faithful Spirit."

In chapter 81:19-23 God describes the transmittance of revelation:

> *That this is in truth the word of an honored messenger (Gabriel), Mighty, established in the presence of the Lord of the Throne, one to be obeyed and trustworthy and your comrade (the Prophet) is not mad. Surely he saw him on the clear horizon.*

These verses show that Gabriel was one of the intimates of God, possessing great power and trust. Again in chapter 40:7 we read, *"Those who bear the power, and all who are around Him, praise their Lord and believe in Him and ask forgiveness for those who believe."* Such characteristics as belief in God and seeking forgiveness from Him are only to be expected from independent, sentient creatures.

In chapter 4:172-173 we read,

> *The Messiah would never disdain to be a servant of God, nor would the angels who are close to Him. He will gather before Him all those who disdain His worship and are arrogant: to those who believe and do good works He will give due rewards and more of His bounty; to those who are disdainful and arrogant He will give an agonizing torment, and they will find no one besides God to protect or help them.*

It is clear that although the Messiah, Jesus, and the favored angels do not disobey the commands of God, they are, nevertheless, warned of a painful punishment on the day of reckoning if they were to commit a wrong. The possibility of neglect of their duties or committing wrong action is necessarily dependent on their being sentient beings, possessed of free will and entrusted with the task of transmitting the revelation of God.

Thus we learn from the Qur'an that Gabriel is the Faithful Soul: he is trustworthy and to be obeyed because he is obeyed by angels in his task. An indication of these obedient angels comes in the verse,

> *No indeed! This [Qur'an] is a lesson from which those who wish to be taught should learn, [written] on honored, exalted, pure pages, by the hands of noble and virtuous scribes. [80:11-16]*

The Angels and the Devils

According to the explanation of contemporary non-Muslim writers, angel is the name given to forces in nature, which represent goodness and happiness, and devils are forces in nature representing evil and unhappiness. What we understand from the Qur'an, however, is that they are beings existing beyond our sense-range, who possess feelings and an independent free-will. To the verses above, (indicating that angels possess independence and free will), may be added many other verses which confirm these same qualities.

The refusal of Satan to prostrate himself before Adam and the dialogue between Satan and God occurs several times in the Qur'an. Satan, after having been expelled from intimacy with God, says in chapter 38:82-83, *"I surely will lead every one of them astray except your sincere slaves among them."* And God replies, *"I shall fill hell with you and with those who follow you, together"* [38:85].

It is clear that punishment can only take place if the punished understand the reason for the punishment. God in chapter 34:20 says in confirmation of Satan's warning to man, *"And Satan indeed found his calculation true concerning them, for they follow them, all except a group of true believers."* Likewise, we read in chapter 14:22, *"And Satan said when the matter had been decided: Indeed! Allah promised you a promise of truth; and I promised you and failed you. And I had no power over you except that I called to you and you obeyed me. So do not blame me but blame yourselves."*

Blame is a matter which can only be associated with those who possess the power of reason and free-will. We quote these verses to show that Satan, like the rest of the angels, is a thinking independent being rather than a force in nature.

Just as verses occur in the Qur'an concerning the angels and the devils, there also are verses which clearly and vividly describe the *jinn* (elemental spirits or invisible beings, either harmful or helpful). In chapter 46:18 reference is made to those who, invited to believe in Islam, spurn it as just another ancient fable or superstition:

> *Such are those in whom the word concerning nations of the jinn and mankind which have passed away before them has effect. Indeed they are the losers.*

We may understand from this verse that *the jinn*, the invisible entities, like mankind, live in different nations, pass a period of time in their different societies and finally die.

In the same chapter, verses 29-32 we read,

> *And when we inclined toward you (Muhammad) certain of the jinn who wished to hear the Qur'an and when*

they were in its presence said, Listen! and, when it was finished turned back to their people warning. They said: O our people! Truly we have heard a book which has been revealed after Moses, confirming that which was before it, guiding to the truth, and a right road, O my people! respond to God's Summoner and believe in Him. He will forgive you some of your wrong actions and guard you from a painful doom. And whoever does not respond to God's Summoner he can in no way escape in the earth, and you (can find) no protecting friends instead of Him. Such are in clear error.

These verses clearly confirm that the *jinn*, like human beings, live in groups, are thinking individuals possessing free will and charged with duties. Moreover, there are other verses dealing with the day of rising which affirms these same qualities in the *jinn*.

The Call of Conscience

According to the explanation of certain modern writers, prophethood is the rising up of a man from amongst his people in order to undertake social reform in accordance with the call of his conscience. The Qur'an, however, gives a different meaning to the prophethood. In 91:7-8 we read, *"And a soul and Him who perfected it, and inspired it (with conscience of) what is wrong for it and (what is) right for it."*

In this verse God demonstrates that each individual perceives from his own conscience and God-given nature the difference between good and bad action; and, that the potential for reform and the bettering of one's self is contained within each person; some listen to their conscience and act correctly while others pay no heed and so act wrongly.

Thus in the following verses, 9-10, of the same chapter God says: *"He is indeed successful who causes it to grow and he is indeed a failure who stunts it."* If prophethood manifests itself as a result of the conscience, which everyone possesses, then everyone in theory may become a prophet. God, however, has reserved this duty for certain men only.

Thus He says in chapter 6:124, *"And when a sign comes to them, they say: we do not believe until we are given that which God's messengers are given. God knows best with whom to place His message."*

The Reality of the Prophet's Mission

We should repeat at this point that we do not intend to prove or disprove here the truth of Islam or the validity of the Prophet's invitation of the people to Islam. Rather, we simply want to state that the second of the modern non-Islamic explanations is also not in accordance with the explanation given in the Qur'an.

According to it, the prophet succeeded in convincing people to believe in a set of superstitions framed in a politico-religious framework; he was aided in this, so they say, by the fact that his own people were tribesmen, having no advanced culture of their own. In the name of public good and the well-being of society harsh punishments were promised to those who did not obey the religious laws; the Prophet instilled a fear of the Day of Reckoning and promised rewards for those who obeyed.

Thus fervor for the promised paradise and fear of the Day of Reckoning created a society based on a religious foundation.

The history of the lives of other prophets has, for the most part, been lost in time, but the life of the Prophet Muhammad is well documented. Anyone who researches into it will not be left in the least doubt that he had total faith and inner certainty in his mission. If religious beliefs were mere superstitions or a means to unify and subdue a society, then all the proofs expounded in the Qur'an concerning the hereafter, the existence of a Creator of the World, Divine Unity, His attributes, belief in a prophecy and the reckoning of a person's actions after death would have absolutely no meaning.

What the Qur'an Says About the Meaning of Revelation and Prophecy

The Qur'an clearly states that it is a book revealed to the Prophet and that revelation is a kind of divine utterance beyond the understanding or communication of the material world; revelation is unperceived by sense or intellect but apprehended by other faculties which, by God's will, are present in certain individuals. Through revelation instructions from the unseen are received and their acceptance and implementation is called prophethood. To clarify this matter we may make the following points.

Man's Innate Nature

In the beginning of this book we explained that each created entity, whether mineral, plant or animal, is endowed with an inherent force which enables it to develop in accordance with its own innate design and nature.

Thus we read in chapter 20:50, *"Our Lord is He who gave everything its nature, then guided it correctly,"* and again in chapter 87:2-3 *"Who creates, then disposes, who measures, then guides."* We also know that man is not excluded from this general law, that is, he has a direction and an aim towards which he develops, having been endowed with faculties which allow him to fulfill this aim. All his happiness lies in achieving this aim; his sorrow, grief and misfortune are the result of his failure to achieve this aim. He is guided to this special purpose by his Creator.

As God says in chapter 76:3, *"Indeed, we have shown him the way whether he be grateful or disbelieving."* Likewise we read in chapter 80:19-20, *"From a drop of seed, He creates him and proportions him. Then makes the way easy for him."*

Man's Path in Traversing the Road of Life

The difference between the animal and plant kingdoms and man is that the former react according to their inherent knowledge or instinct, while man, also possessing an inherent knowledge, is equipped with an intellect and the capacity to use or recognize wisdom. Even if man is capable of undertaking a certain action, he weighs the good or the bad, the benefit or harm, contained in that action and implements it only if he estimates that the benefit outweighs the harm.

Thus he follows the instruction of his intellect in every action; the intellect dictates the necessity of an action. The intellect causes one to abandon an act if it is likely to bring with it an unacceptable degree of trouble and hardship; it not only instructs one on the feasibility of an action, but it also takes into account the dictates of sentiment and feeling.

Indeed the perception of sentiment with regard to the relative good or bad in matter is so closely connected with the decision of the intellect as to be considered one and the same thing.

Man as a Social Being

No one would deny that men are social beings who co-operate with each other to better meet their daily needs. We may wonder, however, whether men desire this co-operation from their natural feelings; are they naturally inclined to undertake an action with others and share an interest in something as a social project?

On one level, man's needs, feelings and desires cause him to act for his own benefit and without regard for the needs and wishes of others. Man uses every means to fulfill his own needs: he uses every kind of transport to reach his destination; he uses the leaves, stems and fruit of plants and trees; he lives upon the meat of animals and their products, and takes advantage of a multitude of other things to complement his own deficiencies in certain respects. Can man, whose state is such that he uses everything he finds to his own ends, be expected to respect another human being? Can he extend his hand to another in co-operation and turn a blind eye to his own desire for the sake of mutual benefit?

The answer in the first instance must be no. It is as a result of man's countless needs, which can never be fulfilled by himself alone, that he recognizes the possibility of fulfilling them through the help and co-operation of others. Similarly, he understands that his own strengths, desires and wishes are also shared by others, and just as he defends his own interests so others defend theirs.

Thus, out of necessity, he co-operates with the social nexus and gives a certain measure of his own efforts to fulfill the needs of others; in return he benefits from the efforts of others in order to fulfill his own needs. In truth he has entered into a market-place of social wealth, always open to traders and offering all the benefits obtained by the collective work of the society. All these factors are placed together in this marketplace of pooled human resources and each person, according to the importance society attaches to his work, has a share in these benefits.

Thus man's first nature incites him to pursue the fulfillment of his own needs using others in the process and taking advantage of their work for his own ends. It is only in cases of necessity and helplessness that he lends a hand to co-operate with society.

This matter is clear when we observe the nature of children: anything a child wants he demands in an extreme way; he emphasizes his demand by crying. As he grows older, however, and becomes a part of the social fabric, he gradually puts an end to his excessive demands. More evidence for the truth of this may be seen when a person accumulates power which exceeds that of others and he rejects the spirit of cooperation and its restrictions of society; such an individual uses people and the fruits of their labors for himself without giving anything back in return.

God refers to the necessary spirit of natural cooperation in society in chapter 43:32, *"We have apportioned among them their livelihood in the life of the world, and raised some of them above others in rank that some of them take labor from others ..."* This verse refers to the reality of the social situation in which each individual has a different capacity and different talents: those who are superior in one domain engage the cooperation or employ of others for their eventual mutual benefit.

Thus all members of society are linked together in the ways and wants of the fabric of one single social unit. Those who do not see the obvious necessity of mutual cooperation are condemned by God in chapter 14:34, *"Truly man is surely a wrong-doer, (a tyrant)"* and, in chapter 33:72, *"Indeed he has proved a tyrant and a fool."*

These verses refer to man's natural instinct which, unless checked, drives him to take advantage of his fellow-men and in doing so to overstep the rights of others.

The Manifestation of Social Differences and the Necessity of Law

Man in his dealings with his fellow men is obliged to accept a social life based on cooperation; in doing so he effectively forgoes some of the freedom enjoyed within his own sphere of work. Merely taking part in a society based on injustice and gaining social differences is not enough to satisfy the basic needs of the average man. In such a society, taking advantage of the efforts of others leads to corruption and a loss of the original purpose of removing glaring differences between men and bettering their lives.

It is clear that a framework of laws, understood and respected by all, must govern the different members of society. If there are no clear laws governing even the most basic of transactions (like buying and selling), transactions will cease to function correctly. Laws are necessary to preserve the rights of individuals. The power and wisdom of the Creator, who has guided man towards his well-being and happiness, has also guaranteed the success and happiness of society.

Guidance in the form of social law is mentioned by God in 80:19-20, *"From a drop of seed He creates him and proportions him. Then makes the way easy for him."* This making of life easy for him is an indication of the social guidance which He has given to man in the form of laws and instructions.

The Intellect is not Sufficient in Guiding Man towards Respect of the Law

The guidance we are considering here is that which emanates from the wisdom of the Creator; this wisdom has created man and allotted him his goal of well-being just as it has assigned a path and goal to all creation. This goal of happiness and well-being is the path of self-fulfillment based on correct behavior in a social setting. It is clear that, of necessity, there can be no inconsistencies or shortcomings in the work of the Creator.

If, at times, one cannot discern His aim or it seems hidden from normal perception, it is not through lack of reason or cause on the part of God, but rather that the cause is linked to other causes which obscure the one in question. If there were no hindrances to a clear perception of the causal chain of events, two given actions would never appear inconsistent or contradictory to the harmony of creation. Nor would the work of the Creator appear (as it sometimes does to those whose perception is hindered by the intricacy of the causal chain of events), inconsistent and imperfect.

Guidance towards the law, whose function is to remove differences and conflict between individuals in society, is not a matter for the intellect since it is this very intellect which causes man to dispute with others. It is the same intellect which incites man to profit at the expense of others and to preserve, first and foremost, his own interest, accepting justice only when there is no alternative.

The two opposing forces, one causing difficulties and one doing away with them, are qualities of man's character; they do not obviously exist in the Creator: the countless daily transgressions and violations of the law, in effect, all result from those who use their intellect incorrectly; they themselves are the very source of their own difficulties.

If the intellect was truly a means of removing wrong action from society and was itself a trustworthy guide to man's well-being, it would recognize the validity of the law and prevent man from violating it. The intellect's refusal to willingly accept what is obviously given for the well-being of man is confirmed when we realize that its acceptance of a society based on just laws is only out of necessity. Without this compulsion, it would never accept to know the law.

Those who transgress the law do so for many reasons: some oppose it without fear, because their power exceeds that of the law; others, because they live outside the reach of the law, through deceit or negligence on the part of the authorities; others are able to invent reasons which make their wrong actions appear lawful and acceptable; some make use of the helplessness of the person they have wronged. All, however, find no legal obstacle in their wrong aims; even if an obstacle appears, their intellect, rather than guiding them to an acceptance of the law, renders the obstacle right and ineffective.

From these examples we are left in no doubt that the intellect, far from controlling, restricting or guiding man, merely uses its influence to its own purpose. We must conclude, therefore, that it is incapable of guiding man towards a social law which guarantees the rights, freedom and well-being of all the members of society.

God says in chapter 96:6-7 *"Indeed man truly rebels when he thinks himself independent."* The independence referred to here includes the independence of those who imagine that they can claim their rights through other than the path of legality.

The Only Way to Guidance is that of Revelation

Man, like the rest of creation, naturally seeks his own well-being and happiness as he lives out his life. Since, by his very make-up, he has a variety of natural needs, he has no alternative but to live in society in order to fulfill these needs; his own well-being and search for the fulfillment of his natural character takes place in the wider framework of society's well-being.

Thus the only acceptable pattern of existence, regulated by a comprehensive law common to all people, is the one which guarantees both the well-being of society and of the individual in a balanced and just fashion. It is also clear that man, like the rest of creation, must endeavor to achieve his well-being and undertake whatever preparation is necessary for achieving this by allowing himself to be guided by his Creator.

It is but a logical next step in our analysis to say that any guidance from the Creator must be towards this comprehensive law, common to all and, at the same time, in accord with the individual's well-being. Intellect is not enough to guide man to the law since it does not always decide in favor of cooperation with others nor in favor of the common good.

The path, the way, which fits perfectly the requirements of man, is the way taught by the Prophets and Messengers of God. It is the way brought to them by God through revelation and established as undeniably true and valid, by the example of their own lives and their intimate knowledge and contact with God.

In chapter 2:213, God says, *"Mankind was one community, and God sent (to them) prophets as bearers of good news and as warners, and revealed to them the book with the truth that it may judge between mankind concerning that in which they differed."* Here we understand "one community" to mean a society at peace, its members living without dispute or difference. After a period of time, men differed with one another and as a result God sent the prophets.

Again, He says in 4:163, 165, *"Indeed we have inspired you as we have inspired Noah . . . Messengers of good news and a warning, in order that mankind might have no argument against God after the Messengers."* Intellect alone does not make man accountable to God and this is why he must be awakened to the reality of his inner condition by other means.

The first of the above-mentioned verses recognizes the way of revelation and prophecy as the only way of removing differences between men. The second shows revelation and prophecy to be the complete and absolute proof to mankind of the truth of God's message.

Some Questions Answered

Question: By using the premise that the intellect cannot prevent violation of the law and the wrong action of man in general, you are declaring the necessity of imposing a law or, as you say, "guidance" towards his own well-being; that is, you are demanding that we place our trust in revelation and in prophethood rather than in the intellect.

The truth is, however, that the laws and instructions of revelation are also ineffective in that they cannot prevent violation of the law, of the Shari`ah law or divine code; in fact, man's acceptance of this code is even less than his acceptance of the civil code. What can you reply to this?

Answer: To point out the way is one thing and to follow it is another. The Creator has taken upon Himself to guide mankind to a law under which he can achieve his well-being; He has not taken upon himself to stop mankind from infringing upon the law nor of compelling men to follow the law. We have investigated above the problem of man's infringement of the law, not to prove that the intellect is deficient or incapable of preventing wrong action but, rather, to show that it usually does not decide in favor of the law or of cooperation with society.

As we have pointed out, the intellect only follows the law out of necessity; if it perceives that obeying the law and restricting one's personal freedom brings less benefit than disobedience, then it will not follow the law nor stop others from transgressing.

The acceptance of the way of the revelation, however, always brings with it obedience to the law. By accepting the code of behavior revealed by the prophets, one entrusts one's judgment to God who, with his boundless power and knowledge, constantly watches over man; only He can reward good deeds or punish bad ones in an absolutely just and unbiased way. God says in chapter 12:40, *"The decision rests with God only,"* and in chapter 99:7-8, *"And whoever does an atom's weight of good will see it then, and whoever does an atom's weight of bad will see it then."*

Likewise, He says in 22:17, *"Indeed God will decide between them on the Day of Rising, Indeed! God is witness over all things,"* and in 2:77, *"Are they unaware that God knows that which they keep hidden and that which they proclaim?"* In 33:52 we read: *"And God is Watcher over all things."*

From these verses it is clear that the divine *deen* of Islam, which has been given to man through revelation, is not capable of preventing transgression of the law any more than the civil law drawn up by men. The machinery of the civil law appoints officials and employees to control and inspect the action of man and also imposes a system of punishment for his offences; this method only works when the law is strong and the crime is discovered.

The divine *deen* is superior to man-made laws or social orders in that control over man is carried out in a very special way, namely, through the vigil of the angels. Moreover, the divine *deen* obliges in every man and woman to enjoin the right and forbid the wrong. All men, without exception, are instructed to watch over the action of their fellow men and to be guardians of the law.

It is only belief in a divine order which contains and defines action outside the limits of good and bad and within the reality of the Day of Reckoning to come. Most importantly, the Lord of the world and of all the unseen world is aware of man's every action and is present with him everywhere at every moment.

Like the civil codes drawn up by man, there is also in the divine code a corresponding system of punishment for every sin, both in this world and on the day of reckoning after death. Unlike the civil code, however, the divine law guarantees that no man will escape from judgment and punishment, if punishment is warranted. As proof, the reader is urged to follow what is written in chapter 4:59, *"Obey God and obey the messenger and those of you in authority"* and, in 9:71, *"And the believers, men and women, are protecting friends one to another; they enjoin the right and forbid the wrong."*

Likewise, we may study 82:10-12 when God says, *"Indeed there are guardians above you, generous and recording, who know (all) that you do"* and, also in 34:21, *"And your Lord (O Muhammad) takes note of all things."*

A Second Question: It has been argued that the intellect does not always decide in favor of respect for the law. Is this not inconsistent with what is contained in the saying of the Imams which states that God has given two proofs to his servants, the outward and obvious one being that of His Prophet, and the inner and hidden one being that of the intellect of man? How are we to understand this statement in the light of how the intellect has been described?

Answer: Without exception, man's intellect is concentrated on securing benefit and avoiding harm. Whenever it accepts to cooperate and share in society's activity, it is, as we have seen above, seeking its own benefit. This need is often felt by those who wish to profit from others or seek to control others by using their wealth. For such men there is nothing prohibiting them from pursuing their illegal action; their intellect will not decide in favor of the law nor forbid transgression of the same law.

If, however, the source of compulsion (as is understood in the light of divine revelation) is from God, then the effect on man is totally different. God's watching over man's action, His punishment or reward of bad or good action, admits of no negligence, ignorance or incapacity. The intellect, which recognizes the existence of God, cannot refuse the law. It will always decide in favor of that which revelation demands of man.

Thus the intellect of a believing man will recognize the importance of the revelation over any personal matter. God say in 13:33 *"Is He who is aware of the deserts of every soul (as he who is aware of nothing?)"* and, in 86:4, *"No human soul but has a guardian over it"* and, 74:38, *"Every soul is a pledge for its own deeds."*

The Path of Revelation is Protected Against Mistakes

The path of revelation is part of the Creator's program. He never makes mistakes, neither in His Creation nor in the system of belief and the laws of the *shari`ah*, which are delineated for man through revelation.

God says in 72:26-28,

> *(He is) the Knower of the Unseen, and He reveals His secret to no one except to every messenger He has chosen, and He makes a guard go before him and a guard behind him, that He may know that they have indeed conveyed the messages of their Lord. He surrounds all their doings and He keeps count of all things.*

From this we understand that the prophets and messengers of God must be infallible both in receiving the revelation and in preserving it against alteration and attack. They are as instruments at the disposal of the Creator's wisdom. Were they to make an error in receiving or teaching the message of the revelation or be led astray by the whispering of evil persons, were they themselves to commit wrong or deliberately change the message they had to deliver, then the wisdom of God would be unable to perfect its program of guidance.

God confirms in chapter 16:9 that He is in total control of man's guidance by means of his messenger, *"And God's is the direction of the way, and some (words) do not go straight."*

The Hidden Reality of Revelation

The reality of revelation is hidden from us. What is clear is that the aim of the program of life, outlined for man by the Creator, cannot possibly have been put together by the intellect; there must be another way of understanding, of perceiving, (other than through reflection and thought), by which man learns of the duties incumbent on him and his fellow human beings. This understanding may only be encompassed by the path of revelation.

There are, however, only a limited number of human beings who possess this kind of understanding since receiving revelation requires an understanding based on purity, sincerity and freedom from all corruption and bad thoughts. It requires people whose spiritual qualities do not change; people who are psychologically balanced in their judgments and who possess real depth of understanding. It must be admitted that these qualities are rarely to be found amongst people.

The Prophets and Messengers mentioned in the Qur'an are men of precisely these qualities. The Qur'an does not mention their number; it only names a few (namely Adam, Nuh (Noah), Hud, Salih (Methusaleh), Ibrahim (Abraham), Lut (Lot), Isma`il (Ismael, Ishmael), Alyasa` (Elisha), Dhu al-Kifl (Ezekiel), Ilyas (Elias), Yunus (Jonah), Idris (Enoch), Ishaq (Isaac), Ya`qub (Jacob), Yusuf (Joseph), Shu`ayb, Musa (Moses), Harun (Aaron), Da'ud (David), Sulayman (Solomon), Ayyub (Job), Zakariya' (Zacharias), Yahya (John), Isma`il Sadiq al-Wa`d, `Isa (Jesus) and Muhammad; others are indicated but not named).

We, as ordinary men, do not share at all their qualities and so we cannot taste the reality of their perception. Prophecy, as an experience, remains unknown for us. Moreover, few of the past revelations have reached us and we have only a limited view of the reality which is revelation and prophecy. It may be that what has reached us in the form of revealed books is exactly as the revelation we are familiar with, that is the Qur'an.

Nevertheless, it is possible that other revelations (completely unknown to us) may have contained information and instructions of which we have no knowledge.

How the Qur'an was Revealed

Qur'anic revelation, according to the Qur'an itself, is an utterance on behalf of God to His Prophet; the Prophet received the speech of God with all his being, not just by way of learning. In 42:51-52 God says,

> *It is not granted to any mortal that God should speak to him except through revelation or from behind a veil, or by sending a messenger to reveal by His command*

> *what He will: He is exalted and wise. So We have revealed a spirit to you [Prophet] by Our command: you knew neither the Scripture nor the faith, but We made it [the Qur'an] a light, guiding with it whoever We will of Our servants. You give guidance to the straight path,...*

On comparison of these two verses we discover three different ways of divine utterance. Firstly, God speaks without there being any veil between Him and man. Secondly, God speaks from behind a veil: like the tree on the *Tur* mountain from behind which Moses heard God speaking. Thirdly, God's speech is brought to man by an angel who had previously heard the revelation from Him.

The second of the two verses above show that the Qur'an has reached us by means of the third of three possible ways. Again God says in 26:192-5, *"Truly, this Qur'an has been sent down by the Lord of the Worlds: the Trustworthy Spirit (Gabriel) brought it down to your heart [Prophet], so that you could bring warning in a clear Arabic tongue,"* and in chapter 2:97 *"Who is an enemy to Gabriel! For it is he who has revealed (this book) to your heart."*

From these verses we understand that the Qur'an was transmitted by way of an angel named Gabriel, or the "Trustworthy Spirit", and that the Prophet received the revelation from him with all his being, all his perception and not merely by listening. The verse says "on your heart," which in Qur'anic terms means perception or awareness. In 53:10-11 we read, *"And He revealed to His slave that which He revealed. The heart did not lie (in seeing) what it saw;"* and in 98:2 reception of the revelation is indicated as a reading of "pure pages" by God's messenger.

Chapter 4

THE RELATIONSHIP OF THE QUR'AN TO THE SCIENCES

Praise of Knowledge and the Stimulation of the Desire to Study

No other revealed book praises and encourages science and knowledge as does the Qur'an and it is for this reason that the Qur'an names the age of the desert Arabs, together with their pagan cultures, before Islam as the "age of ignorance." In over a hundred verses reference is made to science and knowledge in a variety of ways; and many of these verses praise the value of scientific knowledge. In 96:5 God indicates the favor He has done man by bringing him out of his state of ignorance. *"He teaches man what he did not know."*

Likewise, we read in 58:11, *"God will exalt those who believe among you and those who have knowledge to high ranks,"* and in 39:9 God says, *"Are those who know equal to those who do not?"* Besides the many verses in the Qur'an concerning knowledge, there are also countless traditions of the Prophet and the Imams on this subject which rank second only in importance to the Qur'an.

The Sciences which the Qur'an Invites People to Study

In verses too numerous to mention, the Qur'an invites one to reflect upon the signs of creation: the heavens, the shining stars and their astonishing celestial movements, and the cosmic order which rules over them all. Similarly, the Qur'an urges one to reflect upon the creation of the earth, the seas, the mountains, the desert, and the wonders contained below the surface of the earth, the difference between night and day and the changing cycle of seasons. It urges mankind to meditate on the extraordinary creation of the plants and the order and symmetry governing their growth, as well as the multiplicity of the animal kingdom.

The Qur'an invites one to witness the interdependence of beings and how all live in harmony with nature. It calls upon man also, to ponder on his own make-up, on the secrets of creation which are hidden within him, on his soul, on the depth of his perception, and on his relationship with the world of the spirit.

The Qur'an commands man to travel in the world in order to witness other cultures and to investigate the social orders, history and philosophies of past people. Thus it calls man to a study of the natural sciences, mathematics, philosophy, the arts and all sciences available to man, and to study them for the benefit of man and the well-being of society.

The Qur'an recommends the study of these sciences on the condition that it leads to truth and reality, that it produces a correct view of the world based on an understanding of God. Knowledge, which merely keeps a man occupied and prevents him from knowing the reality of his own existence, is equated with ignorance. God says in 30:7, *"They know only some appearance of the life of one world and are heedless of the Hereafter,"* and in chapter 45:23, *"[Prophet], consider the one who has taken his own desire as a god, whom God allows to stray in the face of knowledge, sealing his ears and heart and covering his eyes – who can guide such a person after God [has done this]?"*

The Qur'an not only stimulates the desire for study but is itself a complete system of education of divine knowledge; it provides, too, a model for human behavior and thought. This complete way of life is called *Islam*, the way of submission.

The Sciences Particular to the Study of the Qur'an

There are many sciences devoted to the study of the Qur'an itself. The development of such sciences dates from the first day of Qur'anic revelation; over a period of time they were unified and perfected. Today countless books are available on these sciences, fruit of the labor of different researchers over the centuries.

Some of these sciences investigate the language and vocabulary of the Qur'an, and some the meanings. Those concerned with language are the sciences of correct Qur'anic pronunciation and reading (*tajweed* and *qira'ah*). They explain the simple changes which certain letters undergo when occurring in conjunction with others, the substitution of letters and the places prescribed for breath-pausing, and other similar matters. They also study the different ways the Qur'an has been written down and the several generally accepted ways of recitation, together with the three lesser known ways and the rarer modes of recitation.

Other works enumerate the number of chapters and their verses, while others relate these numbers to the whole Qur'an. They discuss the tradition of Qur'anic calligraphy and how it differs from the normal Arabic script. They research, too, into the meanings of the Qur'an and the general division of subject matter, such as the place and circumstance of revelation, the interpretation of certain verses, the outward and inner meanings, the *muhkam* (clear) or the *mutashabih* (ambiguous), and the abrogating and the abrogated verses.

Others study the verses containing the laws (which, in fact, are part of what is known as Islamic *fiqh* or jurisprudence). Others specialize in the commentary of the meanings (already seen in a previous section of the book). Specialists in each of the different sciences have published numerous works on each subject.

The Sciences which Developed because of the Qur'an

The sciences of the *deen* of Islam came into being at the beginning of the Prophet's mission and the revelation of the Qur'an, including laws governing the behavior and transactions of Muslims. Study of these sciences developed in the first century after the *Hijrah* although initially, not in any formal way. Since the Caliphs had prohibited the writing down of the tradition, they were handed down by word of mouth by the companions and their followers.

A small number of Scholars wrote on jurisprudence and on the science of the traditions at the beginning of the second century when the prohibition was lifted[43], allowing scholars to record the traditions.

It was at this point that a number of disciplines came into being including the Science of Traditions and the Science of establishing the authority and sincerity of those men who transmitted it; the Science of analysis of the text of the traditions; the Science of the foundations of jurisprudence and jurisprudence itself; the Science of belief in the judgment after death and the after-life. Even philosophy, which entered the Islamic arena via the Greek, and remained there for some time in its original Greek, took on the color and beliefs of the people after a time.

Changes in the subject matter and the structure of disciplines took place such that today, amongst Muslims, all subject matter concerning divine gnosis is supported by proofs and reasons taken from the Qur'an and the traditions.

All these subjects were also studied as an integral part of the Arabic language: mastery of the science of verb declension, grammar, meanings of words, commentary and explanation, the art of metaphors and good style, and the philosophy and science of derived meanings allowed greater precision and clarity in the study of the Islamic Sciences as a whole.

Indeed what stimulated scholars to record and arrange coherently the laws of the Arabic language was the sense that they were serving God; love of Him drew them to a clarity and sweetness of style which in turn generated the Science of correct speech and composition.

It is thus related that Ibn `Abbas, who was one of the commentators amongst the companions, explained the meanings of verses by taking examples of the vocabulary

---

43. This restriction was lifted by the Umayyad caliph `Umar ibn `Abd al-`Aziz, 99-101 AH.

in question from Arabic poetry. He advised people to collect and learn Arabic poetry saying,

> *Poetry is the court of the Arabs (meaning the place where the finest language may be heard).*

The famous Shi`ite scholar Khalil ibn Ahmad al-Farahidi wrote the book *al-`Ayn* on the subject of language and also described the science of poetic rhyme.

Many others also wrote on the same subjects. The subject of history was initially derived in Islam from stories of the lives of prophets, in particular that of the Prophet Muhammad, and the description of the course of past nations. To this basic material was added an account of the events during the period immediately following the appearance of Islam. All this was developed into a history of the world in the writings of such men as al-Tabari, al-Mas`udi, al-Ya`qubi and al-Waqidi.

The original reason the Muslims translated and transmitted the natural Sciences and mathematics from other cultures and languages into Arabic was the cultural stimulation given to them by the Qur'an. Many different Sciences were translated from Greek, Syriac and Sanskrit into Arabic.

Access to these sciences was at first available only to the Caliph (who was at that time leader of only Arab Muslims). Gradually they were made available to all Muslims and improved upon as research methods, structuring, classification and ordering of the subjects developed.

One of the main reasons the civilization of Islam, which formed after the death of the Prophet, came to include a large part of the inhabited world (and which today numbers over six hundred million inhabitants[44]), was the Qur'an. We as Shi`ahs, however, deny that the caliphs and the kings who followed them had legitimate claim to the guardianship and execution of the law even though they expanded Islamic civilization, and do not fully agree with the way they explained the realities of Islam.

Indeed the light of wisdom which illuminated the world was from the light of the miracle of the Qur'an. The appearance and diffusion of the revelation caused a change in the direction of history and generated a chain of important events resulting in the progress and development of the culture of man.

---

44. i.e., At the time this book was originally written: the middle of the 20th century.

Chapter 5

THE ORDER OF THE QUR'AN'S REVELATION AND THE GROWTH OF THE QUR'ANIC SCIENCES

The Order in which the Verses of the Qur'an were Revealed

That the chapters and verses were not revealed in one place but rather in stages over a period of twenty-three years during the Prophet's mission is authenticated not only by historical evidence but also from evidence from the various verses. In 17:106 we read: *"it is a recitation that We have revealed in parts, so that you can recite it to people at intervals; We have sent it down little by little."* As further proof there are abrogating and abrogated verses which are directly related to events from different periods and circumstances and which obviously were not revealed at one time.

At this point we should note that the chapters and verses were not revealed in the order in which they are set out; that is the first chapter "al-Fatihah" (The Opening) was revealed after "The Cow", "The Family of `Imran," "Women" and "The Table Spread." This is true also for the order of the verses which do not necessarily follow chronologically. The content of a Qur'anic text may for example show that the content of some chapters and verses concord with the first period of the Prophet's mission – like the chapters "The Clot," and "Nun," but are recorded at the end of the Qur'an.

Many chapters and verses which correspond to the time after the migration like "The Cow," "The Family of `Imran," "Women," "The Spoils" and "Repentance" have been placed at the beginning of the Qur'an.

The contents of the chapters and verses are thus directly related to the events, circumstances and different needs of the period of the Prophet's mission: the chapters and verses which only deal with the calling of the polytheists to belief in God's oneness and the struggle against the idol-worshippers correspond to a time before the migration when the Prophet was inviting the people to Islam in Mecca.

The verses dealing with battles and those dealing with social laws were revealed after the events and circumstances associated with the establishment and progress of the Islamic society in Medina.

Conclusions to be Drawn

We may divide the chapters and Qur'anic verses according to the place, time and circumstance of their revelation:

Some of the chapters and verses are Meccan and some Medinan; usually those revealed before the Prophet's migration are counted as Meccan. The majority of the chapters, and especially the shorter ones, are of this type. Those revealed after the migration are counted as Medinan even though they may have been revealed outside Medina or even in Mecca.

Some chapters and verses were revealed while the Prophet was travelling and some while he was resident in a place. The verses are also divided according to whether they were revealed by day or by night, in peace or in war, or when the Prophet was on earth or in the heavens, or whether he was alone or with others. In the light of these different classifications we may study the reasons for the revelations.

Some chapters were revealed more than once such as the chapter "al-Fatihah," which was revealed once in Mecca and once in Medina. Some verses were revealed several times like, *"Which is it of the favors of your Lord do you deny,"* in the chapter 55, "The Beneficent", which is repeated thirty times, and the verse, *"And indeed your Lord, He is truly the Mighty, the Merciful,"* (e.g., 26:159), which is repeated eight times.

Sometimes one verse occurs in more than one chapter such as *"they say: when is the fulfillment of promise, if you are truthful"* (e.g. 27:71). We find, too, that a sentence appears as a complete verse in one chapter and as part of another verse elsewhere; for example, the sentence, *"Allah! there is no God save Him, The Alive, The Eternal,"* is a complete verse in the beginning of "The Family of `Imran (3:2)." Yet, in "The Cow" it is part of the "al-Kursi" verse (2:255). Most chapters and verses, however, were revealed in one place at one time and do not recur in the Book.

Similar verses appear in different places in the Qur'an because of certain subjects which demand repetition. One of the significant features of the Qur'an is the difference in the length of the chapters. We may compare "Abundance" (the shortest chapter, 108) and "The Cow" (the longest, chapter 2).

Likewise we may compare the length of verses, with the shortest being the single Arabic word *"mudhammatan"* (dark green with foliage) and the longest, composed of thirty sentences being the two hundred and eighty-second verse of "The Cow" (whose subject concerns debt).

All these differences are in accordance with the demands of the revelation. Sometimes it happens that two verses are closely connected in meaning but differ greatly in length; for example, the thirtieth and thirty-first verses of "The Cloaked One (74)", the first being a single sentence and the second more than eleven sentences.

We should not forget that most of the shorter chapters like "The Dawn (89)" and "The Night (92)" are Meccan, and those whose subject matter is treated in greater length and detail are Medinan. The first verse to be revealed to the Prophet was during the revelation of the first five verses of "The Clot (96)" and the last to be revealed was verse 281 of "The Cow (2)": *"And guard yourselves against a day in which you will be brought back to Allah. Then every soul will be paid in full that which it has earned and they will not be wronged."*

The Reasons for the Revelations

Many of the verses are connected with events and circumstances which took place as the Prophet called the people to Islam, for example "The Cow[45]".

---

45. The second chapter (*al-Baqarah*) descended in 1 A.H. in Medina. Some of its verses reproach the Jews who prevented the progress of Islam and others are about the rituals like the five-daily prayers facing the *qiblah*, the month of fasting, hajj, etc.

Other chapters, like "The Exile (59)", refer to the exile of the Banu al-Nadir and the chapter "The Coursers (100)" was revealed for the Bedouin Arabs of the Dry Valley and other tribes. Some chapters or verses were revealed because of the need to explain the laws and directions of Islam; for example, the chapter "The Women (4)" which defined marriage and the inheritance of women, "The Spirits (72)" which explains how to deal with the prisoners-of-war captured as booty and, the chapter "Divorce (65)" which was revealed, as its name suggests, to explain divorce[46].

The circumstances leading to the revelation of these chapters are called "reasons for revelation" and there are countless traditions on this subject.

Amongst the Sunni's there are many traditions which deal with the reasons for revelation; several thousand narrations may be enumerated (although in the Shi`ite School only a few hundred may be counted). Many of these are without a chain of narration and are not accepted as fully trustworthy; moreover, a considerable number are classified as weak. The dubious nature of the majority of these may be ascribed to the following reasons. Firstly, it is obvious from the form of many of these sayings that the narrator had not learned them through oral transmission but rather based on his own judgment, that the revelation of a certain verse was connected with certain events. Thus the narrator links a certain event to a verse of suitable meaning mentioned in the tradition.

This is a subjective view, carried out through *ijtihad* or personal reflection upon the matter, and not the actual reason for revelation learned orally through transmission from the Prophet. As proof of this argument, we may cite

---

46. See *Surah* 4, 8 and 65 respectively.

many inconsistencies amongst these traditions. There are verses, for example, recorded as having several conflicting "reasons for revelation" which are totally unconnected with each other.

Ibn `Abbas, for example, who is not alone in this practice, relates several "reasons for the revelation" of one single verse. The existence of such conflicting reasons is because many have been arrived at through subjective deliberation rather than transmitted directly from the Prophet. This results in one narrator attributing a certain verse to a particular event while another narrator attributes it to another event.

On other occasions a narrator relates two different reasons for the revelation of one verse and thus implicates himself in two conflicting views; then he rejects the first view in favor of the second. We are led to conclude, moreover, that most of these narrations are fabrications or deceitfully transmitted under the pretence of trustworthy narrators. Such doubt concerning the validity of many of these traditions greatly endangers their credibility.

Secondly, it has been related with certainty that the early Caliphs strictly prohibited the recording and writing down of the narrations and, whenever a sheet of paper or tablet was found on which a saying had been written, it was burned. This prohibition lasted until nearly the end of the first century after *Hijrah*, that is, for a period of about ninety years. The effect of this prohibition was that the narrators and scholars of sayings were free to make small additions or changes during oral transmission of the saying. These additions gradually accumulated until the original meaning of the saying was lost.

This becomes very clear on investigation of an event or subject which has been related by two different narrators;

one may come across a saying which describes an event and see the same event described in a different way by another narrator. False sayings were not only introduced by attributing them to respected narrators but also by the hypocrites. Their sayings soon became part of the main body of sayings and this further undermined the credibility of this particular section of the Science of tradition.

The Method Used in Describing "The Reasons for the Revelations"

Past scholars of Islam, and in particular the Sunni scholars, attached great importance to the order of revelation of the chapters. Among the narration on the subject is that of Ibn `Abbas, who has said that *"the beginning of each chapter which was revealed in Mecca was recorded as having been revealed in that very place, then God added what He wanted to it."*[47] The following is the order of revelation of the Qur'an (beginning with the Meccan chapters):

1. *Surat Al-`Alaq* (The Clot) (96)
2. *Surat Al-Qalam* (The Pen) (68)
3. *Surat Al-Muzzammil* (The Enshrouded One) (73)
4. *Surat Al-Muddaththir* (The Cloaked One) (74)
5. *Surat Al-Masad* (The Palm Fiber, Flame) (111)
6. *Surat At-Takweer* (The Overthrowing) (81)
7. *Surat Al-A`laa* (The Most High) (87)
8. *Surat Al-Layl* (The Night) (92)
9. *Surat Al-Fajr* (The Dawn) (89)
10. *Surat Ad-Duhaa* (The Morning Hours) (93)

47. Al-Suyuti, *al-Itqan*, vol. 1, p. 10 (quoting *Fada'il al-Qur'an* of Ibn Daris).

11. *Surat Ash-Sharh* (The Relief) (94)
12. *Surat Al-Humazah* (The Traducer) (103)
13. *Surat Al-`Aadiyaat* (The Courser) (100)
14. *Surat Al-Kawthar* (The Abundance) (108)
15. *Surat At-Takaathur* (The Rivalry in world increase) (102)
16. *Surat Al-Maa`un* (The Small Kindnesses) (107)
17. *Surat Al-Kaafirun* (The Disbelievers) (109)
18. *Surat Al-Feel* (The Elephant) (105)
19. *Surat Al-Falaq* (The Daybreak) (113)
20. *Surat An-Naas* (The Mankind) (114)
21. *Surat Al-Ikhlaaṣ* (The Sincerity) (112)
22. *Surat An-Najm* (The Star) (53)
23. *Surat `Abasa* (He Frowned) (80)
24. *Surat Al-Qadr* (The Power) (97)
25. *Surat Ash-Shams* (The Sun) (91)
26. *Surat Al-Buruj* (The Mansions of the Stars) (85)
27. *Surat At-Teen* (The Fig) (95)
28. *Surat Quraysh* (Quraysh) (106)
29. *Surat Al-Qaari`ah* (The Calamity) (101)
30. *Surat Al-Qiyaamah* (The Resurrection) (75)
31. *Surat Al-Humazah* (The Traducer) (104)
32. *Surat Al-Mursalaat* (The Emissaries) (77)
33. *Surat Qaaf* (The Letter *Qaaf*) (50)
34. *Surat Al-Balad* (The City) (90)
35. *Surat At-Taariq* (The Nightcommer) (86)
36. *Surat Al-Qamar* (The Moon) (54)

37. *Surat Saad* (The Letter *Saad*) (38)
38. *Surat Al-A`raaf* (The Heights) (7)
39. *Surat Al-Jinn* (The *Jinn*) (72)
40. *Surat Yaa-Seen* (*Yaa Seen*) (36)
41. *Surat Al-Furqaan* (The Criterion) (25)
42. *Surat Faatir* (Originator) (35)
43. *Surat Maryam* (Mary) (19)
44. *Surat Ṭaahaa* (*Taa-Haa*) (20)
45. *Surat Al-Waqi`ah* (The Inevitable) (56)
46. *Surat Ash-Shu`araa'* (The Poets) (26)
47. *Surat An-Naml* (The Ant) (27)
48. *Surat Al-Qasas* (The Stories) (28)
49. *Surat Al-Israa'* (The Night Journey) (17)
50. *Surat Yunus* (Jonah) (10)
51. *Surat Hud* (*Hud*) (11)
52. *Surat Yusuf* (Joseph) (12)
53. *Surat Al-Hijr* (The Rocky Tract) (15)
54. *Surat Al-An`aam* (The Cattle) (6)
55. *Surat As-Saaffaat* (Those who set the Ranks) (37)
56. *Surat Luqman* (*Luqmaan*) (31)
57. *Surat Saba'* (Sheba) (34)
58. *Surat Az-Zumar* (The Troops) (39)
59. *Surat Ghaafir* (The Forgiver) (40)
60. *Surat Fussilat* (Explained in Detail) (41)
61. *Surat Ash-Shuraa* (The Consultation) (42)
62. *Surat Az-Zukhruf* (The Ornaments of Gold) (43)
63. *Surat Ad-Dukhaan* (The Smoke) (44)

64. *Surat Al-Jaathiyah* (The Crouching) (45)
65. *Surat Al-Ahqaaf* (The Wind-Curved Sand Hills) (46)
66. *Surat Adh-Dhaariyaat* (The Winnowing Winds) (51)
67. *Surat Al-Ghaashiyah* (The Overwhelming) (88)
68. *Surat Al-Kahf* (The Cave) (18)
69. *Surat An-Nahl* (The Bee) (16)
70. *Surat Nuh* (Noah) (71)
71. *Surat Ibraaheem* (Abraham) (14)
72. *Surat Al-Anbyaa'* (The Prophets) (21)
73. *Surat Al-Mu'minun* (The Believers) (23)
74. *Surat As-Sajdah* (The Prostration) (32)
75. *Surat At-Tur* (The Mount) (52)
76. *Surat Al-Mulk* (The Sovereignty) (67)
77. *Surat Al-Haaqqah* (The Reality) (69)
78. *Surat Al-Ma`aarij* (The Ascending Stairways) (70)
79. *Surat An-Naba'* (The Tidings) (78)
80. *Surat An-Naazi`aat* (Those who drag forth) (79)
81. *Surat Al-Infitaar* (The Cleaving) (82)
82. *Surat Al-Inshiqaaq* (The Sundering) (84)
83. *Surat Ar-Rum* (The Romans) (30)
84. *Surat Al-`Ankabut* (The Spider) (29)
85. *Surat Al-Mutaffifeen* (The Defrauding) (83)
86. *Surat Al-Baqarah* (The Cow) (2)
87. *Surat Al-Anfaal* (The Spoils of War) (8)
88. *Surat Aali `Imraan* (Family of *Imraan*) (3)
89. *Surat Al-Ahzaab* (The Combined Forces) (33)
90. *Surat Al-Mumtahanah* (She that is to be examined) (60)

91. *Surat An-Nisaa'* (The Women) (4)
92. *Surat Az-Zalzalah* (The Earthquake) (99)
93. *Surat Al-Hadeed* (The Iron) (57)
94. *Surat Muhammad* (Muhammad) (47)
95. *Surat Ar-Ra`d* (The Thunder) (13)
96. *Surat Ar-Rahmaan* (The Beneficent) (55)
97. *Surat Al-Insaan* (The Human Being) (76)
98. *Surat At-Talaaq* (The Divorce) (65)
99. *Surat Al-Bayyinah* (The Clear Proof) (98)
100. *Surat Al-Hashr* (The Exile) (59)
101. *Surat An-Nasr* (The Divine Support) (110)
102. *Surat An-Nur* (The Light) (24)
103. *Surat Al-Hajj* (The Pilgrimage) (22)
104. *Surat Al-Munaafiqun* (The Hypocrites) (63)
105. *Surat Al-Mujaadila* (The Pleading Woman) (58)
106. *Surat Al-Hujuraat* (The Rooms) (49)
107. *Surat At-Tahreem* (The Prohibition) (66)
108. *Surat Al-Jumu`ah* (The Congregation, Friday) (62)
109. *Surat At-Taghaabun* (The Mutual Disillusion) (64)
110. *Surat As-Saf* (The Ranks) (61)
111. *Surat Al-Fath* (The Victory) (48)
112. *Surat Al-Maa'idah* (The Table Spread) (5)
113. *Surat At-Tawbah* (The Repentance) (9)

Further Traditions Concerning the Order and Place of Revelation of the Chapters

The tradition of Ibn ʾAbbas mentions one hundred and thirteen chapters, the chapter "al-Fatihah (1)" not being counted among them. There is another saying, related by al-Bayhaqi from ʾIkrimah[48], which enumerates one hundred and eleven chapters, the three chapters "al-Fatihah (1)," "The Heights (7)," and "Counsel (42)" not being mentioned. When al-Bayhaqi relates this same tradition from Ibn ʾAbbas it includes all one hundred and fourteen chapters. The tradition of al-Bayhaqi reckons "The Defrauders (83)" as one of the Medinan chapters in opposition to the other traditions which count it as Meccan. The order mentioned in these two traditions for both the Meccan and Medinan chapters is different from that of other traditions.

Another tradition, related from ʾAli ibn Abi Talhah[49], says: The chapter "The Cow (2)" was revealed in Medina and "The Family of ʾImran (3)," "Women (4)," "The Table Spread (5)," "Spoils of War (8)," "Repentance (9)," "The Pilgrimage (22)," "Light (24)," 'The Clans (33)," "Those Who Deny (109)," "Victory (48)," "Iron (57)," "She That Disputes (58)," "Exile (59)," "She That Is To Be Examined (59)," "The Helpers of Allah (The Ranks) (61)," "Mutual Disillusion (64)," "O Prophet if you divorce women (65)," "O Prophet why do you ban (66)," "The Dawn (89)," "The Night (92)," "We have revealed it in the night of power (97)," "The Clear Proof (98)," "When the earth shakes (99),"

---

48. Al-Suyuti, *al-Itqaan*, vol. 1, p. 10

49. Al-Suyuti, ibid.

"When the help of Allah comes (110)," and the rest of the chapters were revealed in Mecca.

The intention of the tradition seems only to establish the difference between the Medinan and Meccan chapters and to define the order of revelation of the chapters mentioned. The chapters "Table Spread (5)" and "Repentance (9)" are, without doubt, later in revelation than that indicated in this tradition. Moreover, chapters "The Dawn (89)," "The Night (92)," and "The Night of Power (97)," are counted as Medinan chapters, whereas the above tradition counts them as Meccan. Likewise, "The Thunder (13)," "The Beneficent (55)," "Man (76)," "The Congregation (62)," "The Private Apartments (49)" are considered as Meccan, whereas in the above tradition they are counted as Medinan.

In another tradition related by Qatadah[50], "The Cow (2)," "The Family of `Imran (3)," "Women (4)," "The Table Spread (5)," "Immunity (9)," "The Thunder (13)," "The Bee (16)," "The Pilgrimage (22)," "The Light (24)," "The Clans (33)," "Muhammad (47)," "Victory (48)," "The Private Apartments (49)," "Iron (57)," "The Beneficent (55)," "She that disputes (58)," "Exile (59)," "She that is to be Examined (60)," "The Ranks (61)," "The Congregation (62)," "The Hypocrites (63)," "Mutual Disillusion (64)," "Divorce (65)," the first thirteen verses of 'O You Prophet! Why do you ban' (66)," "When the earth Shakes (99)" and "When the help of Allah comes (110)," were revealed in Medina and the rest in Mecca. This tradition is contrary to the previous traditions and, in particular, with regard to the mention of "The Defrauders," "Man," and "The Clear Proof."

This tradition is, however, unacceptable according to the Science of Traditions, being disconnected from direct

---

50. Al-Suyuti, ibid., vol. 1, p.11

transmission from the Prophet. It is also unclear whether Ibn `Abbas learned of the order of revelation from the Prophet himself or from some other unidentified person, or arrived at it by subjective decision.

If the latter is the case, it has no value or authenticity but for himself. It has also no value historically, as Ibn `Abbas did not have close contact with the Prophet. It is obvious that he could not have been present nor a witness to the revelation of all these chapters. Even if we suppose the tradition to be true, it is still not totally acceptable in matters outside the law of the *shari`ah*.

The only way to discover the true order of the chapters, and whether they are Meccan or Medinan, is to examine the content of the chapters and to compare them with the circumstances and social reality before and after the migration. Such a method is effective in certain cases; the content of chapters "Man (76)," "The Coursers (100)," and the "Defrauders (83)" testify to their being Medinan, although some of these traditions only establish them as Meccan.

The Gathering of the Qur'an into One Volume (Before the Death of the Prophet)

The influence of the Qur'an, which was revealed in separate chapters and verses, increased day by day. Its eloquence and miraculous clarity transfixed the Arabs who attached great importance to fine language; they came from far and wide to hear and learn a few verses from the Prophet. However, the notables of Mecca and the leaders of Quraysh, who were idolaters and bitter enemies of the Prophet and of

Islam, tried to prevent the people from getting close to the Prophet; they tried to frighten off the Arabs by telling them the Qur'an was magic.

Despite this people came, unknown to friends, family and servants, in the dark of night to a place near the Prophet's house and listened to the Prophet reading the Qur'an.

The efforts of the early Muslims in listening to, memorizing and recording the Qur'an were stimulated by another motive; they valued the Qur'an as a sacred document, being the word of God; they were also obliged to read the chapter "al-Fatihah (1)" and a portion of another part of the Qur'an during their prayers. It was also the Qur'an through which the Prophet had been commanded to instruct people in the laws of Islam.

This study and devotion to the Qur'an became more ordered and comprehensive after the Prophet emigrated to Medina and formed an independent Muslim community. He ordered a considerable number of the companions to recite the Qur'an and to learn and teach the laws which were being revealed daily. So important was this activity that, according to special permission granted by God in chapter "Repentance (9)," verse 122, these scholars were relieved of their obligation to go to battle.

Since most of the Prophet's companions, (in particular those who had emigrated from Mecca to Medina), were unable to read or write, the Prophet ordered them to learn from the Jewish prisoners-of-war the simple writing of the time. Thus a group of the companions gradually became literate.

Those of this group who engaged in the recitation of the Qur'an, learning by heart the chapters and verses were called *qurraa'* (reciters); it was from amongst this group that forty (some report seventy) died as martyrs in an accident called Bi'r Ma`unah.

The Qur'an was recorded, as it was revealed, on tablets, bones and the wide flat end of the date palm fronds. There is no doubt that most chapters were in use amongst early Muslims since they are mentioned in numerous *sayings* by both Sunni and Shi`ite sources, relating the Prophet's use of the Qur'an as a call to Islam, the making of prayer and the manner of recitation.

Similarly, one comes across names of chapters in traditions which describe the time when the Prophet was still alive, namely the very long chapters and "al-Fatihah (1)".

After the Death of the Prophet

After the death of the Prophet, `Ali who, (according to a tradition of absolute authority), was more knowledgeable of the Qur'an than any other man, retired to his house and compiled the Qur'an in one volume in the order corresponding to its revelation. Before six months had elapsed after the death of the Prophet, the volume was completed and carried by camel to show to other people.

Just about a year after the death of the Prophet, the war of Yamamah took place in which seventy of the reciters were killed and the Caliphs conceived the idea of collecting the different chapters and verses into one volume. They feared that should a future battle take place and the rest of the *qurraa'* be killed, the whole Qur'an would disappear with them.

Thus, on the orders of the Caliph, a group of the *qurraa'* from amongst the companions including Zayd ibn Thabit, collected the chapters and verses (written on tablets, bones and date palm fronds and kept in the Prophet's house or the houses of reciters), and produced several hand-written copies of the complete Book. They then sent copies of this compilation to all areas of the Muslim domain.

After a time, during the rule of the third Caliph, it came to the attention of the Caliph himself that differences and inconsistencies were appearing in the copying down of the Qur'an; some calligraphers lacked precision in their writing and some reciters were not accurate in their recitation.

Since the word of God seemed threatened with alteration, the Caliph ordered that five of the *qurraa'* from amongst the companions, (one of them being Zayd ibn Thabit who had compiled the first volume), produce other copies from the first volume which had been prepared on the orders of the first Caliph and which had been kept with Hafsah, the wife of the Prophet and daughter of the second Caliph.

The other copies, already in the hands of Muslims in other areas, were collected and sent to Medina where, on orders of the Caliph, they were burnt (or, according to some historians, were destroyed by boiling). Thus several copies were made, one being kept in Medina, one in Mecca, and one each sent to Shaam (a territory now divided into Syria, Lebanon, Palestine and Jordan), Kufa and Basra.

It is said that beside these five, one copy was also sent to Yemen and one to Bahrein. These copies were called the Imam copies and served as original for all future copies. The only difference of order between these copies and the first volume was that the chapters "Spoils of War (8)" and "Immunity (9)" were written in one place between "The Heights (7)" and "Jonah (10),"

The Importance Muslims Attached to the Qur'an

As we have pointed out above, the verses and chapters of the Qur'an were in oral use amongst Muslims at the time of its first and second compilation into one volume. They were extremely careful in preserving what they had learnt by heart.

Moreover, a large group of companions and their followers were engaged only in recitation and learning the Qur'an by heart. The collecting together of the Qur'an into one volume took place under their scrutiny. They all accepted, without objection, the volume when it was given to them and then made copies of it.

It happened that when some men tried to record verse 34 in "Repentance (9)," *"And those who hoard up gold and silver"* without the "and" in the `Uthmanic (second compilation) volume, they were prevented from doing so. The companion Ubayy ibn Ka`b swore that if anyone left out the "and" he would fight him with the sword.

As a result, the word "And" was recorded. One day the second Caliph, during the time of his own caliphate, read the verse,

> *And the first to lead the way of the Muhaajirun and Ansaar and those who follow them in goodness [9:100]*

without the word "and"; he was opposed and forced in the end to read it with the "and".

The Qur'an that had been compiled by `Ali was rejected by several people when he showed it to them. Despite this, `Ali made no objection or resistance and accepted the Qur'an in circulation for as long as he lived, even during the time of his own Caliphate.

Likewise, the Imams of the Prophet's family, the successors and progeny of the Prophet, did not mention their objection to the Qur'an to the intimates amongst their Shi`ite followers. They always referred to the Qur'an in common use and in their commentaries and ordered the followers to recite it as the people did.

`Ali's silence in the matter of the difference of order between the two volumes was in keeping with the preference of the Shi`ite Imams for commentary of the Qur'an by the Qur'an; for them the order of the Medinan and Meccan chapters has no influence on the meanings of the Qur'an; commentary of each verse is made by comparing it to another group of verses. Moreover the Qur'an is eternal and valid for all times and places; such local and temporary particularities as the time, place and circumstances of revelation can have no effect on the higher scale of meanings contained in the Qur'an.

It is true that there are benefits to be gained by knowing certain details of revelation; they help one to discern the development of divine wisdom, social laws or stories of the past prophets and nations; also an understanding of the reasons for revelation show how the call to Islam progressed during the twenty-three years of the Prophet's mission.

We would like to make clear, however, that it was in order to preserve the unity of the Muslims that caused the Shi`ites to be silent in this matter.

The Qur'an is Protected from any Alteration

The transmission of the Qur'an, from the day of its revelation up to the present day, is flawless. The chapters and verses have been in constant use amongst Muslims and have been passed on perfectly intact from one generation to the other. The Qur'an we know today is the same Qur'an which was revealed to the Prophet some fourteen centuries ago.

The Qur'an does not stand in need of historical proof for its identity or authenticity, (although history too confirms its validity). Since a book which claims to be the actual unalterable word of God and attests to this in its own text, does not need to resort to others to prove its authenticity.

The clearest proof that the Qur'an we have with us today is the same that was revealed to the Prophet and that no alteration has taken place in its text is that very superiority which the Qur'an claimed for itself at the time of its revelation and which still exists. The Qur'an says that it is a book of light and guidance, a book which shows man the truth and reality of existence; it says that it explains all things, that is, everything necessary for man to live in accordance with his own natural character; it says that it is the word of God and challenges man and *jinn* to produce similar words; it invites them to find someone like the Prophet, who could neither read nor write and grew up in an age of ignorance as an orphan without instruction; the Qur'an challenges them to find any inconsistency in its method, Sciences, or laws, such as one might find in any ordinary book. They obviously cannot for the superiority of the Qur'an remains after its revelation.

Likewise, the guidance for man contained in the Qur'an is still valid; it still expounds a complete world view which is in accord with the purest of intellectual proofs and is the source of man's well being in this world and in the next. By the benevolence and care shown by the Creator for His creation in the Book, it still invites man to belief.

The Qur'an cares for the needs of man by giving him a vision of reality based on Divine Unity. All knowledge and belief spring from this view of reality. At no point does the Qur'an fail to explain in the most comprehensive fashion the reality of this oneness.

It devotes much attention to explaining the behavior and transactions expected of the individual in society and shows how correct action is that which accords with the natural character and capability (*fitrah*) of man. The Qur'an leaves the detailed description of man's behavior to the Prophet whose daily life was an example of how man was to apply what was contained in the Qur'an.

Together the Book of God and the example (or *Sunnah*) of the Prophet delineated an astoundingly comprehensive life-pattern for man, namely, the way of living in tune with the reality which is Islam. The Qur'an deals precisely with all aspects of individual and social life and, despite having been revealed in another age, does not contain the slightest inconsistency or incompatibility even today. It describes a *deen*, a comprehensive way of life, whose program of living is beyond the imagination of the world's most capable lawyers and sociologists.

The miracle of the Qur'an has in it clarity and eloquence, rooted, as it is, in the language of a nation famed for the purity and power of its language. The Qur'an is a miraculous sun whose light shines far brighter than the finest poetry of the time, indeed of any age. During the Islamic conquests of the first century after Hijra, the resulting admixing of non-Arabic words with the Arabic lessened the purity of Arabic language used in the Qur'an causing it to disappear from the every-day speech of the people.

The Qur'an does not merely challenge man by the use of its language, but also by the depth of its meaning. Those familiar with the Arabic language (both prose and verse writings) are reduced to silence and astonishment when they attempt to describe it.

The Qur'an is neither poetry nor prose but rather seems to draw qualities from both; it is more attractive and dazzling than poetry and clearer and more flowing than prose. A single verse or phrase from the Qur'an is more illuminating, more penetrating, and more profound than the complete speech of most eloquent speakers.

The profundity of meaning in the Qur'an remains as miraculous as ever; its complex structure of beliefs, morals and laws stands as proof that the Qur'an is the word of God. Man, and in particular someone who was born and raised in circumstances similar to those of the Prophet, could never have created such a system; the Qur'an is a harmonious whole despite having been revealed during twenty-three years in greatly varying circumstances.

God Himself confirms that the Qur'an has been preserved from change; in chapter 15:9 He says, *"Indeed We, even We, reveal the Reminder and indeed We are truly its guardian,"* and in chapter 41:41-42, He says, *"for indeed it is an unassailable Book. Falsehood cannot come at it from before or behind it. (It is) a revelation from the Wise, the Owner of Praise."* Only a divine Book could remain preserved for fourteen centuries in a world where the enemies of truth and of Islam are numerous.

The Recitation, Memorization and Transmission of the Qur'an

There were a number of reciters engaged in learning and teaching the Qur'an in Medina. Anyone learning from one of them would transmit that individual's particular style of recitation when he transmitted it to others as a tradition. Various ways of recitation occurred. One may attribute this, firstly, to the fact that the script used at the time was the Kufic style and had no diacritical points; each word could be read in various ways.

Secondly, most people were illiterate and, when learning the Qur'an, had no alternative but to commit it to memory and transmit it orally. This method continued to be used for many generations.

The Different Groups of Reciters

The first group of reciters were those companions who were engaged in learning and teaching the Qur'an during the time of the Prophet. Among them was a group which mastered the whole Qur'an; one of this group member was a woman by the name of Umm Waraqah bint `Abd Allah ibn Harith.

Study was also undertaken by four of the Ansars (or helpers, that is Medinans who became Muslim and welcomed the Muslims from Mecca). They learned the whole Qur'an by heart but were not concerned with the ordering of the verses and chapters; other scholars were responsible for memorization of the order.

Some traditions say that the position of each verse and chapter was defined at the orders of the Prophet himself but this is generally refuted by the rest of the traditions.

According to some later scholars, (namely al-Suyuti in his book *al-Itqaan*, in the chapter dealing with the qualities of the men responsible for transmission), several of the *qurra'* became famous, among them `Uthman, `Ali, Ubayy ibn Ka`b, Zayd ibn Thabit, `Abd Allah ibn Mas`ud and Abu Musa al-Ash`ari.

The second group of reciters were the students of the first group. They were generally *taabi`un* (followers of the companions of the Prophet) and the more famous amongst them had centers of recitation and teaching in Mecca, Medina, Kufa, Basra and Shaam. The `Uthmanic volume was used in these five places.

In Mecca were `Ubayd ibn `Amir and `Ata' ibn Abi Rabah, Ta'us, Mujahid, `Ikrimah ibn Abi Mulaykah and others. In Medina were Ibn Musayyib, `Urwah, Saalim, `Umar ibn `Abd al-`Aziz, Sulayman ibn Yasar, `Ata' ibn Yasar, Mu`adh al-Qari', `Abd Allah ibn al-A`raj, Ibn Shihab al-Zuhri, Muslim ibn Jundub and Zayd ibn Aslam.

In Kufa were `Alqamah, al-Aswad, Masruq, `Ubaydah, `Amr ibn Shurahbil, Harith ibn al-Qays, `Amr ibn Maymun, Abu `Abd al-Rahman al-Sulami, Zarr ibn Hubaysh, `Ubayd ibn Naflah, Sa`id ibn Jubayr, al-Nakha`i, al-Sha`bi, Abu al-`Aliyah, Abu al-Raja' Nasr ibn al-`Asim, Yahya ibn Ya`mur, Hasan al-Basri, Ibn Sirin, Qatadah, Mughirah ibn Abi Shihab, `Uthman, Khalifah ibn Sa`d, Abu Darda'.

The third group lived during the first half of the second century after *Hijrah*; it included a number of Imams famous for their Qur'anic recitation who received this knowledge from the second group. In Mecca were `Abd Allah ibn

Kathir (one of the seven *qurraa'*), Humayd ibn Qays al-A'raj and Muhammad ibn Abi Muhaysin. In Medina were, Abu Ja'far Yazid ibn al-Qa'qa', Shaybah ibn Nassah and Nafi ibn Nu'aym (one of the seven *qurraa'*).

In Kufa were Yahya ibn Waththab, 'Asim ibn Abi al-Najjud (one of the seven *qurraa'*), Sulayman al-A'mash, Hamzah (one of the seven *qurraa'*) and al-Kisa'i (also one of the seven reciters). In Basra were 'Abd Allah ibn Abi Ishaq, 'Isa ibn 'Umar, Abu 'Amr ibn al-'Ala' (one of the seven reciters), 'Asim al-Jahdari and Ya'qub al-Hadrami. In Shaam 'Abd Allah ibn 'Amir (one of the seven reciters), 'Atiyah ibn Qays al-Kalla'i, Isma'il ibn 'Abd Allah ibn Muhajir, Yahya ibn Harith and Shurayh ibn Yazid al-Hadrami.

The fourth group consisted of the students of the third group, like Ibn 'Ayyash, Hafs and Khalaf and many of the most famous may be classed in the next section.

The fifth group comprised those concerned with academic research and writing including Abu 'Ubayd Qasim ibn Salaam, Ahmad ibn Jubayr al-Kufi and Isma'il ibn Ishaq al-Maliki from the companions of Qalun al-Rawi. Included also are Abu Ja'far ibn Jarir al-Tabari and Mujahid. The field of research was widened after them by men like al-Dani[51] and al-Shatibi[52] who wrote a great number of books on poetry.

The Seven Reciters

Seven members of the third group achieved considerable celebrity; they became a focus of learning for others. Each of the reciters appointed two narrators who each propagated

---

51. Abu 'Amr 'Uthman ibn Sa'id al-Dani al-Andalusi, the author of many works including *Kitab al-taysir*, died in 444 A.H.

52. Al-Qasim ibn Firruh al-Shatibi, a famous reciter and author of the celebrated *al-Qasidah al-Shatibiyah* (1120 verses), died 590 A.H. (*Kashf al-Zunun*)

a particular style of recitation. The following is a list of these seven:

First Ibn al-Kathir,[53] whose narrators were Qanbal and al-Bazzi, with only one intermediate narrator in the chain from Ibn `Abbas from the leader of the Faithful, `Ali. The second was Nafi`[54] and his narrators Qalun and Warsh. The third was `Asim[55] and his narrators were Abu Bakr Shu`bah ibn al-`Ayyash and Hafs; the Qur'an recitation which is in common use among Muslims today is according to the reading of `Asim by a narration of Hafs. The fourth was Hamzah[56] and his narrators were Khalaf and Khallad. The fifth was al-Kisa'i[57] and his narrators were al-Dawri and Abu `Ali al-Harith. The sixth was Abu `Amr ibn al-`Ala'[58]; and his narrators al-Dawri and al-Susi with one intermediate narrator. The seventh was Ibn `Amir[59] and his narrators were Hisham[60] and Ibn Dhakwan with one intermediary narrator.

---

53. `Abd Allah ibn Kathir al-Makki (d. 120 A.H.) received his instruction in the recitation of the Qur'an from `Abd Allah ibn al-Sa'ib and Mujahid.

54. Nafi` ibn `Abd al-Rahman ibn Nu`aym al-Isfahani al-Madani (d. 159 or 169 A.H.) received his instruction from Yazid ibn al-Qa`qa` and Abu Maymunah Mawla Umm Salmah.

55. `Asim ibn Abi al-Najjud al-Kufi (d. 127 or 129 A.H.), a pupil, in the art of Qur'anic recitation, of Sa`d ibn Ayyas al-Shaybani and Zarr ibn Hubaysh.

56. Hamzah ibn Habib al-Zayyat al-Tamimi al-Kufi (d. 156 A.H.) was a pupil of `Asim, A`mash, al-Sabi`i and Mansur ibn al-Mu`tamar. He also studied under the Sixth Imam al-Sadiq and was the first to write about the *mutashabihat* of the Qur'an.

57. `Ali ibn Hamzah ibn `Abd Allah ibn Fayruz al-Farisi (d. between 179-193 A.H.), a grammarian and reciter of the Qur'an, was a teacher of the Caliphs al-Amin and al-Ma'mun. He studied grammar under Yunus al-Nahwi and Khalil ibn Ahmad al-Farahidi and Qur'anic recitation under Hamzah and Shu`ba ibn `Ayyash.

58. Abu `Amr Zabban ibn al-`Ala' al-Basri (d. between 154-159 A.H.).

59. `Abd Allah ibn `Amir al-Shafi`i al-Dimashqi (d. 118 A.H.) studied under Abu al-Darda' and the companions of `Uthman.

60. There are differences of opinion as to the names of *ruwah* (transmitters/narrators) of Ibn `Amir. Those mentioned above are given according to al-Suyuti's *al-Itqan*.

Following the seven famous recitations are the three recitations of Abu Ja`far[61], Ya`qub[62] and Khalaf[63].

The majority of Scholars recognize the seven types of recitation as *mutawatir*, that is, as having been related in unbroken chains of transmissions. One group of narrators has equated the tradition that the Qur'an was revealed in seven *harf* (literally, "word" in Arabic), with the seven different recitations; this tradition is well known amongst Muslim scholars in general but is not recognized as being trustworthy[64].

Al-Zarkshi[65] says in his book *al-Burhan*, *"It is true that these seven recitations from the seven reciters have come to us via unbroken chain of transmission but their chain of transmission from the Prophet are open to inspection, since the chains of transmission of the seven reciters are all of the type of single transmission, that is, related by one single man to another single man."*

Al-Makki says in his book, *"Anyone who imagines that the recitation of such men as Nafi` and `Asim are the same seven 'harf' mentioned in the saying of the Prophet is committing a grave mistake."* Moreover, the implication of this saying is that recitations, other than these seven, are not correct; this also is a grave mistake since early Islamic Scholars like Abu `Ubayd al-Qasim ibn Salam and Abu Hatim al-Sijistani, Abu

---

61. Abu Ja`far Yazid ibn al-Qa`qa` al-Madani (d. between 128-133 A.H.), a freed slave of Umm Salmah, received his instruction in Qur'anic recitation from `Abd Allah ibn `Ayyash, ibn `Abbas and Abu Hurayrah.

62. Ya`qub ibn Ishaq al-Basri al-Hadrami (d. 205 A.H.) was a scholar and reciter on the authority of Salam ibn Sulayman, `Asim al-Sulami and `Ali ibn Abi Talib.

63. Khalaf ibn Hisham al-Bazzaz (d. 229 A.H.) was a *rawi* (narrator/transmitter) of Hamzah. He studied under Malik ibn Anas and Hammad ibn Zayd and his pupil was Abu `Awanah.

64. See al-Majlisi, *Bihar al-Anwar* (section on Qur'an); al-Fayd al-Kashani, *al-Safi* (introductory matter); al-Suyuti, *al-Itqan*, vol. 1, p. 47.

65. Al-Suyati, op. cit., vol. 1, p. 82.

Ja'far al-Tabari and Isma'il al-Qadi have recorded several other recitations besides these seven.

At the beginning of the second century A.H. the people of Basra used the recitation of Abu 'Amr and Ya'qub and in Kufa the recitations of Hamzah and 'Asim. In Shaam they used that of Ibn 'Amir and in Mecca that of Ibn Kathir. In Medina that of Nafi' was used. This situation remained unchanged until the beginning of the third century A.H. when Ibn Mujahid removed the name of Ya'qub and put the name of al-Kisa'i in his place.

The reason why scholars paid so much attention to the seven reciters, despite there being many others of equal or better standing, was that the number of recitations had multiplied so quickly that they lost interest in learning and recording all the traditions about recitation. Thus they decided to choose several of the recitations which complied with the orthography of the Qur'an and which were easier to learn and record.

Thus for the five copies of the Qur'an which 'Uthman had sent to the towns of Mecca, Medina, Kufa, Basra and Shaam, five reciters were chosen from the five areas and their recitations were then used. Ibn Jubayr writes about these five recitations from the five forms. Ibn Mujahid records a tradition which asserts that 'Uthman sent two other copies to Yemen and Bahrain, that the number of 'Uthman copies thus numbered seven and that they chose seven narrators.

Since precise information about this tradition (which states that copies were sent to Yemen and Bahrain) was not available, they added two of the reciters of Kufa, to make up the number they had previously chosen, to seven. This number, which corresponds with the above-mentioned saying and affirmed that the Qur'an was revealed in seven recitations, was then used by others who had no knowledge of the matter. They mistakenly supposed that what was meant by the seven *harf* which the Prophet spoke of, was the seven recitations. The only trustworthy recitations are those whose text is sound and whose meaning corresponds to what is written in the Qur'an.

Al-Qurab says in his *al-Shafi*, *"We should look for the seven recitations amongst the* qurraa' *not from among others,"* This view is neither tradition nor *Sunnah* but rather it originated from some of the later scholars who collected the seven recitations. These seven recitations became so well known that people imagined that other recitations should not be used. This however, has never been claimed.

The Number of Verses in the Qur'an

The enumeration and delineation of the verses date from the time of the Prophet. In a saying the Prophet mentions ten verses from the "Family of `Imran (3)," seven in the chapter "al-Fatihah (1)" and thirty in the chapter "The Sovereignty (67)."

There are six views concerning the total number of verses in the Qur'an, as related by al-Dani. Some have said that the total is 6,000, some 6,204 and some 6,219. From these six estimations, two are from the reciters of Medina and four from the other areas to which the `Uthmanic copies were sent, namely, Mecca, Kufa, Basra and Shaam.

All these scholars support their claims by traditions reaching back to the companions and thus not directly linked, in a chain of transmissions, to the Prophet. Such traditions are called *mawquf* in the science of the traditions.

From Medina, those who specialized in enumeration and delineation of the verses, were Abu Ja`far Yazid ibn al-Qa`qa`, Shaybah ibn Nassah, Isma`il ibn Ja`far ibn Abi Kathir al-Ansari, Ibn Kathir, Mujahid, Ibn `Abbas, Ubayy ibn Ka`b, Hamzah, al-Kisa`i, Khalaf, Ibn Abi Layla, Abu `Abd al-Rahman al-Sulami, `Ali, `Asim ibn al-`Ajjaj al-Jahdari, Ibn Dhakwan, Hisham ibn `Ammar.

The reason for the different opinions concerning the total number of verses is related to the method of delineation and separation of the verses and letters.

The Names of the Chapters

The division of the Qur'an into chapters, like its division into verses, is mentioned in the Qur'an itself. In several places God uses the actual words *surah* and *ayat*. In (24:1) He says *"(Here is) a surah which we have revealed,"* in "Repentance (9)", verse 86, *"And when a surah is revealed,"* in "The Cow (2)" verse 23, *"Then produce a surah like it . . ."* and other similar verses.

The name of the chapter is sometimes derived from a name or form occurring in the chapter or from a subject treated by the chapter; for example "The Cow (2)", "The Family of `Imran (3)", "The Night Journey (17)" and "The Unity (112)". We may note here that in the old copies of the Qur'ans it is usual to observe the following at the beginning of each chapter: *"The surah in which the Cow is mentioned"* or *"the surah in which the family of `Imran is mentioned."* Sometimes the chapter becomes known by its first phrase; take for example, the chapter *"Read in the name of your Lord"* (or "the Clot (96)") or the chapter, *"Truly we revealed it"* ("The

Night of Power (97)") or the chapter *"Those who disbelieve"* (also called "The Clear Proof (98)").

Sometimes the chapter becomes known by a certain position or quality it possesses; thus the chapter "The Opening of the Book" or "The Mother of the Book" or "The Seven Oft-repeated verses" (all describing the first chapter, or the "al-Fatihah"). The chapter "The Unity (112)" is also called by the name "al-Ikhlas" (meaning that it describes the absolute unity of God) or by the name "Nisbat al-Rabb" (meaning the chapter which describes the divine nature of the Lord in relation to the slave). This method of naming the chapters was also used in the early days of Islam and is attested to by the traditions.

There are traditions, whose chains of authority reach back to the Prophet, which assert that the names of such chapters as "The Cow (2)", "The Family of `Imran (3)", "Hud (11)" and "The Event (56)" were used by the Prophet himself. We may conclude from this that many of these names came into being at the time of Prophet as a result of being in common use.

Calligraphy, Orthography and Diacritical Marks Used in the Qur'an

The first and second copies of the Qur'an were written in Kufic script at the time of the Prophet. The very basic nature of the script, without diacritical marks, was suitable for the reciters, narrators and scholars who had learned the Qur'an by heart, since only they knew the precise pronunciation of the words. Others found great difficulty if they opened the Book and tried to read correctly.

It was for this reason that at the end of the first century after *Hijrah* Abu al-Aswad al-Du'ali[66], one of the companions of `Ali, with the guidance of the latter, wrote out the rules of the Arabic language and on the orders of the Umayyad Caliph `Abd al-Malik produced a Qura'nic text with diacritical marks. This, to a certain extent, removed the difficulty of reading the Kufic script.

Several difficulties remained, however; the diacritical marks for vowels, for example, were for a time only points. Instead of a *fathah*, a point was placed at the beginning of the letter and, instead of *kasrah*, a point below and, for a *dammah*, a point above at the end of a letter. This led to ambiguity. It was not until Khalil ibn Ahmad al-Farahidi set about explaining the *maddah*, i.e. the lengthening of certain words, the doubling of letters, the diacritical marks of vowelling and the pause, that the difficulty of reading the script was finally removed.

---

66. Al-Suyuti, op. cit., vol. 2, p. 171.

About
`ALLAMAH SAYYID M. H. TABATABA`I

`Allamah Sayyid Muhammad Husayn Tabataba`i – may God shower His blessings upon his soul – was one of the great masters of the traditional sciences in Iran during the 20th century. He was born in 1903 into a distinguished family of scholars in Tabriz, where he also carried out his earliest religious studies. Like many Shi`ite scholars, he pursued more advanced studies in Najaf and then returned to Tabriz. But in 1945, following the Soviet occupation of Azerbaijan, he came to Qum, where he settled until his death in 1982. From this centre of Shi`ite learning the light of his knowledge and presence began to disseminate, and continued to spread, among students not only of that city but also throughout Iran, and even beyond...

More in the Foreword of this book.

www.ingramcontent.com/pod-product-compliance
Lightning Source LLC
Chambersburg PA
CBHW051652040426
42446CB00009B/1103